EMAIL
JOKE BOOK

WILLIS AND WEBBO

The World's Greatest
EMAIL JOKE BOOK

JOHN BLAKE

Published by John Blake Publishing Ltd,
3, Bramber Court, 2 Bramber Road,
London W14 9PB, England

www.blake.co.uk

First published in paperback in 2005

ISBN 1 84454 091 X

All rights reserved. No part of this publication may be reproduced, stored in a retrieval system, or in any form or by any means, without the prior permission in writing of the publisher, nor be otherwise circulated in any form of binding or cover other than that in which it is published and without a similar condition including this condition being imposed on the subsequent publisher.

British Library Cataloguing-in-Publication Data:

A catalogue record for this book is available from the British Library.

Design by www.envydesign.co.uk

Printed in Great Britain by Bookmarque

1 3 5 7 9 10 8 6 4 2

© Text copyright Jon Webster and Nick Davis

Papers used by John Blake Publishing are natural, recyclable products made from wood grown in sustainable forests. The manufacturing processes conform to the environmental regulations of the country of origin.

About the authors

Webbo (aka Jon Webster) has worked for two people in his life: himself and Richard Branson. The former paid better. During a career at Virgin Records, Jon worked with huge-selling artists such as Genesis, Boy George and Ivor Cutler as well as inventing the Now! That's What I Call Music brand and the Mercury Music Prize. He is a Gemini, and both halves live in Hertfordshire with his partner and two children. He likes jokes better than he tells them.

Willis (aka Nick Davis) is a record producer who has worked with many international artists, including Phil Collins, Bjork, AHA, Genesis, Mike and the Mechanics, Deep Purple, Tears for Fears and many others. He has seen and heard more studio goings-on than he cares to remember. He is now married with two children and lives in Hampshire.

⇨ **Acknowledgements**

Nick would like to thank: Alan, Tim Y, Jonathan, Jo, Gill, Philip, Siobhan, Mat, Mikey, Pete, Tim F, Bryan, Tony, Keith Anne-Marie, Annie, Sophie and, of course, Webbo for all the endless laughs they have sent me on a daily basis via my computer.

Jon would like to thank: all the people on my joke-e-mail circulation list (particularly Nick) who have contributed to this book; everyone who doesn't know me; and Mike Lawrence, for being the best teller of jokes I've ever met.

And Aggie Bond.

Contents

Introduction	ix
Battle of the Sexes	1
Music	57
Politics	63
Blondes	77
Health	89
Professional Life	97
Animals	127
Testing Times	135
Religion	159
Technical Support	181
Brotherly Love	197
General Smut	229
It's a Mad World	227
Sports	297
Travel	317

Introduction

Willis and Webbo have been e-mailing each other jokes for more than five years, and in this book they have amassed some of the best jokes ever sent. Blondes, computers, footballers, lawyers, politicians — a whole host of subjects make up this fantastic collection of funnies, which also provides a humorous insight into current affairs.

We hope you enjoy it.

IMPORTANT: This e-mail joke book is intended for the use of the reader and may contain information that is confidential, privileged or unsuitable for overly sensitive persons with low self-esteem, no sense of humour or irrational religious beliefs. If you are not the intended recipient, any dissemination, distribution or copying of this e-mail joke book is not authorised (either explicitly or implicitly) and constitutes an irritating social faux pas.

Unless the word 'absquatulation' has been used in its correct context somewhere other than in this warning, it does not have any legal or grammatical use and may be ignored. No animals were harmed in the transmission of this e-mail joke book, although the pit bull next door is living on borrowed time, let me tell you.

Those of you with an overwhelming fear of the unknown will be gratified to learn that there is no hidden message revealed by reading this warning backwards, so just ignore that Alert Notice from Microsoft. However, by pouring a complete circle of salt around yourself and your computer, you can ensure that no harm befalls you and your pets. If you have received this e-mail joke book in error, please add some nutmeg and egg whites, whisk and place in a warm oven for 40 minutes.

⇝ Battle of the Sexes

———————— Original Message ————————

From: webbo
To: willis
Sent: Monday, December 11, 2000 1:00 PM
Subject: FW: A good question that just had to be asked

Jennifer visited a psychic of some local repute. In a dark and hazy room, peering into a crystal ball, the mystic delivered grave news: 'There's no easy way to say this, so I'll just be blunt – prepare yourself to be a widow. Your husband will die a violent and horrible death this year.'

Visibly shaken, Jennifer stared at the woman's lined face, then at the single flickering candle, then down at her hands. She took a few deep breaths to compose herself. She simply had to know. She met the fortune-teller's gaze, steadied her voice and asked, 'Will I be acquitted?'

THE WORLD'S GREATEST EMAIL JOKE BOOK

---————— Original Message ——————---

From: webbo
To: willis
Sent: Monday, October 22, 2001 5:15 PM
Subject: FW: Coma

A woman is in a coma. Nurses are in her room giving her a sponge bath. One of them is washing her "private area" and notices that there is a response on the monitor when he touches her. They go to her husband and explain what happened, telling him, 'Crazy as this sounds, maybe a little oral sex will do the trick and bring her out of the coma.' The husband is sceptical, but they assure him that they'll close the curtains for privacy. Besides it's worth a try.

The hubby finally agrees and goes into his wife's room. After a few minutes the woman's monitor flat-lines ... no pulse ... no heart rate. The nurses run into the room. The husband is standing there, pulling up his pants and says, 'I think she choked.'

BATTLE OF THE SEXES

———————— Original Message ————————

From: webbo
To: willis
Sent: Friday, October 25, 2002 12:16 PM
Subject: FW: Horses

A man is sitting reading his newspaper when his wife sneaks up behind him and whacks him on the head with a frying pan.

'What was that for?' he asks.
'That was for the piece of paper in your trouser pockets with the name Mary Ellen written on it,' she replies.
'Don't be silly,' he says. 'Two weeks ago, when I went to the races, Mary Ellen was the name of one of the horses I bet on.'
She seems satisfied at this, and she apologises.
Three days later he's again sitting in his chair reading when she nails him with an even bigger frying pan, knocking him out cold.
When he comes around, he asks again, 'What was that for?'
She responds, 'Your f**king horse phoned.'

▣ ☰ THE WORLD'S GREATEST EMAIL JOKE BOOK ☰ ᄆ ᄇ

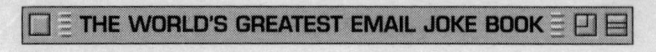

---------- Original Message ----------

From: webbo
To: willis
Sent: Tuesday, February 11, 2003 10:16 PM
Subject: FW: Marital compatibility

An elderly couple had been dating for some time. Finally they decided it was time for marriage. Before the wedding, they went out to dinner and had a long conversation regarding how their marriage might work. They discussed finances, living arrangements and so on. Finally the old gentleman decided it was time to broach the subject of their physical relationship. 'How do you feel about sex?' he asked, rather trustingly.

'Well,' she said, responding very carefully, 'I'd have to say I would like it infrequently.' The old gentleman sat quietly for a moment. Then, peering over his glasses, casually looked her in the eye and asked, 'Was that one or two words?'

BATTLE OF THE SEXES

---------- Original Message ----------

From: willis
To: webbo
Sent: Friday, August 08, 2003 1:03 PM
Subject: FW: Secret code cracked

Words and gestures that women use:

Fine
This is the word women use to end an argument when they feel they are right and you need to shut up. Never use 'fine' to describe how a woman looks — this will cause you to have one of those arguments.

Five minutes
This is half an hour. It is equivalent to the five minutes that your football game is going to last before you take out the rubbish, so it's an even trade.

Nothing
This means 'something', and you should be on your toes. 'Nothing' is usually used to describe the feeling a woman has of wanting to turn you inside out and upside down. 'Nothing' usually signifies an argument that will last 'five minutes' and end with 'fine'.

Go ahead (with raised eyebrows)
This is a dare. One that will result in a woman getting upset over 'nothing' and will end with the word 'fine'.

THE WORLD'S GREATEST EMAIL JOKE BOOK

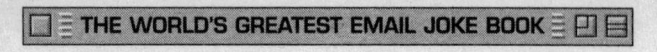

Go ahead or whatever (normal eyebrows)
This means 'I give up' or 'Do what you want because I don't care.' You will get a 'raised eyebrows go ahead' in just a few minutes, followed by 'nothing' and 'fine', and she will talk to you in about 'five minutes' when she cools off.

Loud sigh
This is not actually a word, but a non-verbal statement often misunderstood by men. A 'loud sigh' means she thinks you are an idiot at that moment, and wonders why she is wasting her time standing here and arguing with you over 'nothing'.

Soft sigh
Again, not a word, but a non-verbal statement. A 'soft sigh' means that she is content. Your best bet is not to move or breathe, and she will stay content.

That's OK
This is one of the most dangerous statements that a woman can make to a man. 'That's OK' means that she wants to think long and hard before paying you back for whatever it is that you have done. 'That's OK' is often used with the word 'fine' and in conjunction with 'raised eyebrows'.

BATTLE OF THE SEXES

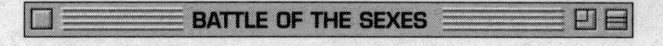

Go ahead
At some point in the near future, you are going to be in some mighty big trouble.

Please do
This is not a statement, it is an offer. A woman is giving you the chance to come up with whatever excuse or reason you have for doing whatever it is that you have done. You have a fair chance with the truth, so be careful and you shouldn't get a 'That's OK'.

Thanks
A woman is thanking you. Do not faint. Just say, 'You're welcome.'

Thanks a lot
This is much different from 'Thanks'. A woman will say, 'Thanks a lot' when she is really ticked off at you. It signifies that you have offended her in some callous way, and will be followed by the 'loud sigh'. Be careful not to ask what is wrong after the 'loud sigh', as she will only tell you 'nothing'.

THE WORLD'S GREATEST EMAIL JOKE BOOK

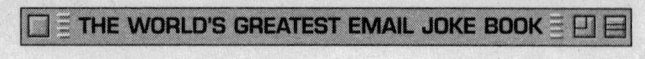

———————— Original Message ————————

From: willis
To: webbo
Sent: Tuesday, April 17, 2001 12:58 PM
Subject: FW: We are what we eat: dangers in food

A dietician was once addressing a large audience in Chicago:
'The material we put into our stomachs is enough to have killed most of us sitting here, years ago. Red meat is awful. Soft drinks erode your stomach lining. Chinese food is loaded with MSG. Vegetables can be disastrous, and none of us realises the long-term harm caused by the germs in our drinking water. But there is one thing that is the most dangerous of all — and we all have, or will, eat it. Can anyone here tell me what food it is that causes the most grief and suffering for years after eating it?'

A 75-year-old man in the front row stood up and said, 'Wedding cake.'

BATTLE OF THE SEXES

--------- Original Message ---------

From: willis
To: webbo
Sent: Wednesday, March 28, 2001 10:23 AM
Subject: Anniversary

A guy says, 'For our 20th anniversary, I'm taking my wife to Australia.' His friend says, 'That's going to be tough to beat. What are you going to do for your 25th anniversary?' The first guy says, 'I'm going to go back and get her.'

THE WORLD'S GREATEST EMAIL JOKE BOOK

---—————— Original Message ——————---

From: webbo
To: willis
Sent: Tuesday, January 09, 2001 1:26 PM
Subject: FW: Satan pays a visit

One bright and beautiful Sunday morning, everyone in the tiny town of Johnstown got up early and went to the local church. Before the service started, the townspeople were sitting in their pews and talking about their lives, their families, etc. Suddenly, the Devil himself appeared at the front of the congregation. Everyone started screaming and running for the front entrance, trampling each other in a frantic effort to get away from evil incarnate.

Soon everyone was evacuated from the church except for one elderly gentleman who sat calmly in his pew, not moving, seemingly oblivious to the fact that God's ultimate enemy was in his presence.

Now this confused Satan a bit, so he walked up to the man and said, 'Don't you know who I am?'
The man replied, 'Yep, sure do.'
Satan asked, 'Aren't you afraid of me?'
'Nope, sure ain't,' said the man.
Satan was a little perturbed at this and queried, 'Why aren't you afraid of me?'
The man calmly replied, 'Been married to your sister for over 48 years.'

```
┌──────────────────────────────────────────────┐
│ ▢  ════════  BATTLE OF THE SEXES ════════ 🗔🗏 │
└──────────────────────────────────────────────┘

─────────────── Original Message ───────────────

**From:** webbo
**To:** willis
**Sent:** Friday, February 23, 2001 12:16 PM
**Subject:** FW: The mother-in-law pays a visit
```

The mother-in-law unexpectedly stopped by a recently married couple's house one day. She rang the doorbell and stepped into the house, and saw her daughter-in-law standing naked by the door. 'What are you doing?' she asked.

'I'm waiting for my husband to come home from work,' the daughter-in-law answered.

'But you're naked!' the mother-in-law exclaimed.
'This is my love dress,' the daughter-in-law explained.
'Love dress? But you're naked!'

'My husband loves me to wear this dress! It makes him happy and it makes me happy. I would appreciate it if you would leave because he will be home from work any minute.'

The mother-in-law was tired of the romantic talk and left. On the way home she thought about the love dress. When she got home she got undressed, showered, put on her best perfume and waited by the front door.

THE WORLD'S GREATEST EMAIL JOKE BOOK

Finally her husband came home. He walked in and saw her standing naked by the door. 'What are you doing?' he asked.
'This is my love dress,' she replied.
'Needs ironing!'

BATTLE OF THE SEXES

—————— Original Message ——————

From: webbo
To: willis
Sent: Friday, March 31, 2000 1:09 PM
Subject: Chain letter

This chain letter was started in hopes of bringing relief to other tired and discouraged men. Unlike most chain letters, this one does not cost anything. Just send a copy of this letter to five of your friends who are equally tired and discontented. Then bundle up your wife or girlfriend and send her to the man whose name appears at the top of the list, and add your name to the bottom of the list. When your turn comes, you will receive 15,625 women. One of them is bound to be better than the one you already have. At the writing of this letter, a friend of mine had already received 184 women, four of whom were worth keeping.

REMEMBER – this chain brings luck. One day a man forwarded this letter and the next day he received the woman who had been named Chest of the Year by the local restaurant chain. An unmarried Melbourne man was able to choose between a massage therapist and a nymphomaniac chef. You can be lucky, too, but don't break the chain! One man broke the chain and he got his ex-wife back.

THE WORLD'S GREATEST EMAIL JOKE BOOK

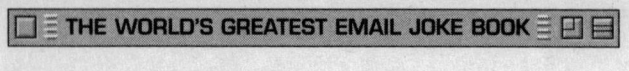

---------- Original Message ----------

From: webbo
To: willis
Sent: Saturday, April 26, 2003 7:53 PM
Subject: Marriage

My wife and I were happy for 20 years. Then we met.

I bought my wife a new car. She called and said, 'There is water in the carburettor.'
I asked her, 'Where's the car?' She replied, 'In the lake.'

The secret of a happy marriage remains a secret.

When a man steals your wife, there is no better revenge than to let him keep her.

I haven't spoken to my wife in 18 months – I don't like to interrupt her.

Getting married is very much like going to a restaurant with friends. You order what you want, then when you see what the other fellow has, you wish you had ordered that.

Man is incomplete until he is married. Then he is finished.

There was a man who said, 'I never knew what real happiness was until I got married; then it was too late.'

BATTLE OF THE SEXES

A man placed an ad in the classifieds: 'Wife wanted.' The next day he received a hundred letters. They all said the same: 'You can have mine.'

A woman was telling her friend, 'I made my husband a millionaire.' 'And what was he before you married him?' asked the friend. 'A billionaire,' she replied.

A man, upon his engagement, went to his father and said, 'Dad! I've found a woman just like Mother.' His father replied, 'So what do you want? Sympathy?'

Eighty per cent of married men cheat in America. The rest of them cheat when they are in Europe.

Marriage is the triumph of imagination over intelligence. Second marriage is the triumph of hope over experience.

If you want your spouse to listen and pay strict attention to every word you say, talk in your sleep.

I married Miss Right. I just didn't know her first name was Always.

It's not true that married men live longer than single men. It only seems longer.

A man was complaining to a friend: 'I had it all – money, a beautiful house, a big car, the love of a beautiful woman – and then, BAM, it was all gone!' 'What happened?' asked his friend. 'My wife found out…'

Just think, if it weren't for marriage, men would go through life thinking they had no faults at all.

The most effective way to remember your wife's birthday is to forget it once.

BATTLE OF THE SEXES

--- Original Message ---

From: webbo
To: willis
Sent: Monday, February 21, 2000 9:58 PM
Subject: FW: Who said women can't follow directions?

MI6 had an opening for an assassin. After all the background checks, interviews and tests were done, there were three finalists — two men and a woman.

For the final test, the MI6 agents took one of the men to a large metal door and handed him a gun. 'We must know that you will follow your instructions, no matter what the circumstances. Inside this room, you will find your wife sitting in a chair. Kill her!' The man said, 'You can't be serious. I could never shoot my wife.' The agent said, 'Then you're not the right man for this job.'

The second man was given the same instructions. He took the gun and went into the room. All was quiet for about five minutes. Then the man came out with tears in his eyes. 'I tried, but I can't kill my wife.' The agent said, 'You don't have what it takes. Take your wife and go home.'

Finally, it was the woman's turn. She was given instructions to kill her husband. She took the gun and went into the room. Shots were heard, one shot after another. They heard screaming, crashing, banging on the walls. After a few minutes, all was quiet. The door opened slowly and there stood the woman. She wiped the sweat from her brow and said, 'You guys didn't tell me the gun was loaded with blanks. I had to beat him to death with the chair.'

BATTLE OF THE SEXES

———————— Original Message ————————

From: willis
To: webbo
Sent: Friday, October 04, 2002 10:29 AM
Subject: Old couple

A little old couple walked slowly into McDonald's one cold winter evening. They looked out of place amid the young families and young couples eating there that night. Some of the customers looked admiringly at them. You could tell what the admirers were thinking: 'Look, there's a couple who have been through a lot together, probably for 60 years or more!' The little old man walked right up to the cash register, placed his order with no hesitation and then paid for their meal.

The couple took a table near the back wall and started taking food off of the tray. There was one plain hamburger, one order of French fries and one drink. The old man unwrapped the hamburger and carefully cut it in half. He placed one half in front of his wife. Then he carefully counted out the fries, divided them into two piles and neatly placed one pile in front of his wife. He took a sip of the drink, then his wife took a sip and set the cup down between them. As the man began to eat his few bites of hamburger, the crowd began to get restless. Again you could tell what they were thinking: 'That poor old couple. All they can afford is one meal for the two of them.'

THE WORLD'S GREATEST EMAIL JOKE BOOK

As the man began to eat his fries, one young man stood and came over to the old couple's table. He politely offered to buy them another meal. The man replied that they were just fine – they were used to sharing everything. Then the crowd noticed that the lady hadn't eaten a bite. She just sat there, watching her husband eat and occasionally taking turns sipping the drink.

Again the young man came over and begged them to let him buy them something to eat. This time the lady explained that, no, they were used to sharing everything with each other. As her husband finished eating and was wiping his face neatly with a napkin, the young man could stand it no longer. Again he came over to their table and offered to buy some food. After being politely refused again, he finally asked the old lady, 'Ma'am, why aren't you eating? You said that you share everything. What is it that you are waiting for?' She answered, 'The teeth.'

BATTLE OF THE SEXES

---------- Original Message ----------

From: webbo
To: willis
Sent: Saturday, July 05, 2003 12:42 AM
Subject: Dear John Letter

A marine stationed in Afghanistan recently received a Dear John Letter from his girlfriend back home. It read as follows:

Dear Ricky,
I can no longer continue our relationship. The distance between us is just too great. I must admit that I have cheated on you twice since you've been gone, and it's not fair to either of us. I'm sorry. Please return the picture of me that I sent to you.
Love, Becky

With hurt feelings, the marine asked his comrades for any snapshots they could spare of their girlfriends, ex-girlfriends, sisters, aunts, cousins, and so on. In addition to the picture of Becky, Ricky included all the other pictures of the pretty girls he had collected from his mates. There were 57 photos in that envelope, along with this note:

THE WORLD'S GREATEST EMAIL JOKE BOOK

Dear Becky,
I'm so sorry, but I can't quite remember who you are. Please take your picture from the pile, and send the rest back to me.
Take care, Ricky

——————— Original Message ———————

From: webbo
To: willis
Sent: Friday, August 18, 2000 12:32 PM
Subject: FW: Bad luck

A woman's husband had been slipping in and out of a coma for several months, yet she had stayed by his bedside every single day. One day, when he came to, he motioned for her to come nearer. As she sat by him, he whispered, eyes full of tears, 'You know what? You have been with me all through the bad times... When I got fired, you were there to support me. When my business failed, you were there. When I got shot, you were by my side. When we lost the house, you stayed right here. When my health started failing, you were still by my side... You know what?'
'What dear?' she asked gently, smiling as her heart began to fill with warmth.
'I think you're bad luck. Why don't you f**k off.'

BATTLE OF THE SEXES

---— Original Message ———

From: willis
To: webbo
Sent: Thursday, July 08, 2004 1:54 PM
Subject: Newsflash

'A scientist from Monash University in Melbourne, Australia, has invented a bra that keeps women's breasts from jiggling and prevents the nipples from pushing through the fabric when cold weather sets in. At a news conference announcing the invention, a large group of men took the scientist outside and kicked the shit out of him.'

---— Original Message ———

From: willis
To: webbo
Sent: Friday, August 25, 2000 5:15 PM
Subject: FW: One for the lads

A man is happily driving home one night when he's pulled over by the police. The policeman approaches him and asks, 'Have you been drinking, sir?'
'Why?' asks the man. 'Was I all over the road?'
'No,' replies the policeman, 'you were driving splendidly. It was the fat, ugly bird in the passenger seat that gave it away.'

THE WORLD'S GREATEST EMAIL JOKE BOOK

─────────── Original Message ───────────

From: webbo
To: willis
Sent: Monday, October 09, 2000 4:35 PM
Subject: FW: Men fight back...

How many men does it take to open a beer?
None. It should be opened by the time she brings it.

Why is a launderette a really bad place to pick up a woman?
Because a woman who can't even afford a washing machine will never be able to support you.

Why do women have smaller feet than men?
So they can stand closer to the kitchen sink.

How do you fix a woman's watch?
You don't. There's a clock on the stove!

Why do men pass gas more than women?
Because women won't shut up long enough to build up pressure.

If your dog is barking at the back door and your wife is yelling at the front door, whom do you let in first?
The dog, of course... At least he'll shut up after you let him in.

BATTLE OF THE SEXES

All wives are alike, but they have different faces so you can tell them apart.

What do you call a woman who has lost 95% of her intelligence?
Divorced.

Bigamy is having one wife too many. Some say monogamy is the same.

Marriage is a three-ring circus: engagement ring, wedding ring and suffering.

The last fight was my fault. My wife asked, 'What's on the TV?' I said, 'Dust!'

In the beginning, God created earth and rested. Then God created man and rested. Then God created woman. Since then, neither God nor man has rested.

My wife and I are inseparable. In fact, last week it took four police officers and a dog.

Why do men die before their wives?
They want to.

What is the difference between a dog and a fox?
About five drinks.

A beggar walked up to a well-dressed woman shopping in Rodeo Drive, Beverly Hills, California, and said, 'I haven't eaten anything in four days.' She looked at him and said, 'God, I wish I had your willpower.'

What is the punishment for bigamy?
Two mother-in-laws.

Young son: 'Dad, I heard that in some parts of Africa a man doesn't know his wife until he marries her? Is it true?'
Dad: 'That happens in every country, son.'

First guy (proudly): 'My wife's an angel!'
Second guy: 'You're lucky. Mine's still alive.'

BATTLE OF THE SEXES

---------- Original Message ----------

From: willis
To: webbo
Sent: Wednesday, January 17, 2001 12:50 PM
Subject: FW: 30 harsh things a woman can say to a naked man - rated R

1. I've smoked fatter joints than that.
2. Ahh, it's cute.
3. Why don't we just cuddle?
4. You know, they have surgery to fix that.
5. Make it dance.
6. Can I paint a smiley face on it?
7. Wow and your feet are so big.
8. It's OK, we'll work around it.
9. Will it squeak if I squeeze it?
10. Oh no, a flash headache…
11. (Giggles and points.)
12. Can I be honest with you?
13. How sweet, you brought incense.
14. This explains your car.
15. Maybe if we water it, it'll grow.
16. Why is God punishing me?
17. At least this won't take long.
18. I never saw one like that before.
19. But it still works, right?
20. It looks so unused.
21. Maybe it looks better in natural light.
22. Why don't we skip straight to the cigarettes?

THE WORLD'S GREATEST EMAIL JOKE BOOK

23. Are you cold?
24. If you get me really drunk first…
25. Is that an optical illusion?
26. What is that?
27. It's a good thing you have so many other talents.
28. Does it come with an air pump?
29. So this is why you're supposed to judge people on personality.
30. I guess this makes me the 'early bird'.

BATTLE OF THE SEXES

――――――― Original Message ―――――――

From: webbo
To: willis
Sent: Monday, March 31, 2003 10:50 PM
Subject: Austin Powers chat-up lines

1. I wish you were a door so I could bang you all day long.
2. (Lick finger and wipe on her shirt): Let's get you out of those wet clothes.
3. Nice legs... What time do they open?
4. Do you work for the post office? I thought I saw you checking out my package.
5. You've got 206 bones in your body. Want one more?
6. Can I buy you a drink, or do you just want the money?
7. I may not be the best-looking guy in here, but I'm the only one talking to you.
8. I'm a birdwatcher and I'm looking for a Big-Breasted Bed Thrasher. Have you seen one?
9. I'm fighting the urge to make you the happiest woman on earth tonight.
10. Wanna play army? I'll lie down and you can blow the hell outta me.
11. I'd really like to see how you look when I'm naked.
12. You might not be the best-looking girl here, but beauty is only a light switch away.
13. You must be the limp doctor because I've got a stiffy.

THE WORLD'S GREATEST EMAIL JOKE BOOK

14. I'd walk a million miles for one of your smiles, and even further for that thing you do with your tongue.
15. If it's true that we are what we eat, then I could be you by morning.
16. (Look down at your crotch): Well, it's not just going to suck itself.
17. You know, if I were you, I'd have sex with me.
18. You, me, whipped cream and handcuffs. Any questions?
19. Those clothes would look great in a crumpled heap on my bedroom floor.
20. My name is (name)... Remember that, you'll be screaming it later.
21. Do you believe in love at first sight or should I walk by again?
22. Hi, the voices in my head told me to come over and talk to you.
23. I know milk does a body good, but DAMN, how much have you been drinking?
24. Do you sleep on your stomach? Can I?
25. Do you wash your pants in Mr Sheen, because I can see myself in them?

BATTLE OF THE SEXES

---— Original Message ———

From: webbo
To: willis
Sent: Tuesday, September 12, 2000 9:39 AM
Subject: Jokes

If the dove is the bird of peace, what is the bird of true love?
The swallow.

How do you annoy your girlfriend during sex?
Phone her.

Why do women fake orgasms?
Because they think men care.

What is the definition of 'making love'?
Something a woman does while a guy is shagging her.

What should you do if your girlfriend starts smoking?
Slow down and use a lubricant.

What's the difference between oral sex and anal sex?
Oral sex makes your day; anal sex makes your hole weak.

What's the difference between premenstrual tension and BSE?
One's mad cow disease, the other's an agricultural problem.

If your wife keeps coming out of the kitchen to nag at you, what have you done wrong?
Made her chain too long.

How do you turn a fox into a dog?
Marry it!

What is the difference between a battery and a woman?
A battery has a positive side.

What are the three fastest means of communication?
1) Internet
2) Telephone
3) Telawoman

Why do hunters make the best lovers?
Because they go deep in the bush, shoot more than once and they eat what they shoot.

What's the connection between fat girls and mopeds?
You don't mind riding them, but you don't want your mates to find out.

What's the connection between a woman and a condom?
Both of them spend more time in your wallet than on your dick.

BATTLE OF THE SEXES

What should you give a woman who has everything?
A man to show her how to work it.

How are tornadoes and marriage alike?
They both begin with a lot of blowing and sucking, and in the end you lose your house.

Why does a bride smile when she walks up the aisle?
She knows she's given her last blow job.

What's the difference between a bitch and a whore?
A whore sleeps with everyone at the party and a bitch sleeps with everyone at the party except you.

What's the difference between your wife and your job?
After 10 years the job still sucks.

What's the difference between love, true love and showing off?
Spitting, swallowing and gargling.

Do you know why they call it the Wonder Bra?
When you take it off, you wonder where her tits went.

THE WORLD'S GREATEST EMAIL JOKE BOOK

———————— Original Message ————————

From: willis
To: webbo
Sent: Monday, September 25, 2000 5:00 PM
Subject: FW: Livestock show

A man takes his wife to the livestock show. They start heading down the alley that houses all the bulls. The sign on the first bull's stall states: 'This bull mated 50 times last year.' The wife turns to her husband and says, 'He mated 50 times in a year, isn't that nice!' They proceed to the next bull and his sign states: 'This bull mated 65 times last year.' The wife turns to her husband and says, 'This one mated 65 times last year. That's over five times a month. You could learn from this one!' They proceeded to the last bull and his sign says, 'This bull mated 365 times last year.' The wife's mouth drops open and she says, 'WOW! He mated 365 times last year. That's ONCE A DAY!!! You could really learn from this one.' The fed-up man turns to his wife and says, 'Go up and enquire if he had to f**k the same cow every day.'

BATTLE OF THE SEXES

---— Original Message ———

From: willis
To: webbo
Sent: Monday, October 13, 2003 8:20 PM
Subject: Mirrors never lie

A husband and wife are getting ready for bed. The wife is standing in front of a full-length mirror taking a hard look at herself. 'You know, love,' she says, 'I look in the mirror and I see an old woman. My face is all wrinkled, my boobs are barely above my waist, my bum is hanging out a mile, I've got fat legs and my arms are all flabby.' She turns to her husband and says, 'Tell me something positive to make me feel better about myself.' He thinks about it for a bit and then says, 'Well, there's nothing wrong with your eyesight, love.'

THE WORLD'S GREATEST EMAIL JOKE BOOK

———————— Original Message ————————

From: willis
To: webbo
Sent: Monday, December 15, 2003 12:28 PM
Subject: FW: Life's pleasures

A man was walking down the street when a particularly dirty and shabby-looking homeless man accosted him, and asked him for a couple of pounds for dinner. The man took out his wallet, pulled out £5 and asked, 'If I give you this money, will you buy some beer with it instead?' 'No, I had to stop drinking years ago,' the homeless man replied.

'Will you use it to gamble instead of buying food?' the man asked. 'No, I don't gamble,' the homeless man said. 'I need everything I can get just to stay alive.'

'Will you spend the money on greens fees at a golf course instead of food?' the man asked.

'Are you MAD?!' replied the homeless man. 'I haven't played golf in 20 years!'

'Will you spend the money on a woman in the red-light district instead of food?' the man asked.

'What disease would I get for five lousy quid?!' exclaimed the homeless man.

'Well,' said the man, 'I'm not going to give you the money. Instead, I'm going to take you home for a terrific dinner cooked by my wife.'

The homeless man was astounded. 'Won't your wife be

furious with you for doing that? I know I'm dirty, and I probably smell pretty disgusting.'

The man replied, 'That's OK. I just want her to see what a man looks like who's given up beer, gambling, golf and sex.'

THE WORLD'S GREATEST EMAIL JOKE BOOK

---— Original Message ———

From: webbo
To: willis
Sent: Sunday, June 18, 2000 7:47 AM
Subject: FW: Marriage or prison?

A woman woke in the middle of the night to find her husband missing from their bed. In the stillness of the house, she could hear a muffled sound downstairs. She went downstairs and looked all around, still not finding her husband. Listening again, she could definitely hear moaning. She went down to the basement to find her husband crouched in the corner facing the wall, sobbing. 'What's wrong with you?' she asked him.

'Remember when your father caught us fooling around when you were 16?' he replied. 'And remember, he said I had two choices: I could either marry you, or spend the next 20 years in prison.'

Baffled, she said, 'Yes, I remember. So?'

'I would have got out today.'

BATTLE OF THE SEXES

---— Original Message ———

From: willis
To: webbo
Sent: Monday, December 04, 2000 3:14 PM
Subject: FW: Honeymoon

A young Jewish couple got married and went off on their honeymoon. When they got back, the bride immediately called her mother.

'Well,' said her mother, 'so how was the honeymoon?'

'Oh, Mama,' she replied, 'the honeymoon was wonderful! So romantic...' Suddenly she burst out crying. 'But, Mama, as soon as we returned Sam started using the most horrible language – things I'd never heard before! I mean, all these awful four-letter words! You've got to come get me and take me home ... PLEASE, MAMA!'

'Sarah, Sarah,' her mother said, 'calm down! Tell me, what could be so awful. WHAT four-letter words?'

'Please don't make me tell you, Mama,' wept the daughter. 'I'm so embarrassed, they're just too awful! COME AND GET ME, PLEASE!'

'Darling, baby, you must tell me what has you so upset. Tell your mother these horrible four-letter words!'

Still sobbing, the bride said, 'Oh, Mama ... words like dust, wash, iron, cook...'

'I'll pick you up in 10 minutes,' said the mother.

THE WORLD'S GREATEST EMAIL JOKE BOOK

―――――― Original Message ――――――

From: webbo
To: willis
Sent: Tuesday, December 05, 2000 9:24 PM
Subject: FW: One for the girls...

A woman was out golfing one day when she hit her ball into the woods. She went to look for it and found a frog in a trap. The frog said to her, 'If you release me from this trap, I will grant you three wishes.' The woman freed the frog and the frog said, 'Thank you, but I failed to mention that there was a condition to your wishes: that whatever you wish for, your husband will get 10 times more or better!' 'That would be OK,' said the woman, and for her first wish she wanted to be the most beautiful woman in the world. The frog warned her, 'You do realise that this wish will also make your husband the handsomest man in the world – an Adonis that women will flock to?' 'That will be OK,' replied the woman, 'because I will be the most beautiful woman and he will only have eyes for me.' So, bing! She's the most beautiful woman in the world! For her second wish, she wanted to be the richest woman in the world. The frog said, 'That will make your husband the richest man in the world and he will be 10 times richer than you.' 'That will be OK,' said the woman, 'because what is mine is his, and what is his is mine.' So, bing! She's the richest woman in the world! The frog then enquired about her third wish,

BATTLE OF THE SEXES

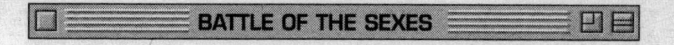

and she answered, 'I'd like a mild heart attack.'
Moral of the story: Women are clever b*tches. Don't mess with them!

| ☐ ≡ **THE WORLD'S GREATEST EMAIL JOKE BOOK** ≡ 🗐 🗏 |

---————— Original Message ——————---

From: webbo
To: willis
Sent: Tuesday, December 12, 2000 1:16 PM
Subject: Hello from the sunshine state

A couple went on holiday to a fishing resort in Scotland. The husband liked to fish at the crack of dawn. The wife liked to read. One morning the husband returned after several hours of fishing and decided to take a short nap. Although the wife wasn't familiar with the lake, she decided to take the boat. She rowed out a short distance, anchored and returned to reading her book. Along came the local official in his boat. He pulled up alongside her and said, 'Good morning, madam. What are you doing?'

'Reading my book,' she replied, as she thought to herself, 'Isn't it obvious?'

'You're in a restricted fishing area,' he informed her.

'But I'm not fishing. Can't you see that?'

'Yes, but you have all the equipment. I'll have to take you in.'

'If you do that, I'll have to charge you with rape,' snapped the irate woman.

'But I haven't even touched you,' replied the official.

'That's true,' she replied, 'but you do have all the equipment.'

```
╔══════════ BATTLE OF THE SEXES ══════════╗
```

─────────── Original Message ───────────

From: willis
To: webbo
Sent: Friday, December 15, 2000 11:09 AM
Subject: FW: The perfect husband

There are several men sitting around in the changing room of a private club after exercising. Suddenly a mobile phone rings. One of the men picks it up, and the following conversation ensues:

'Hello?'

'Darling, it's me. Are you at the club?'

'Yes.'

'Great! I'm at the shopping arcade round the corner and I just saw a beautiful mink coat. It's absolutely gorgeous! Can I buy it?'

'How much?'

'Only £8,000.'

'Well, OK, go ahead and get it if you like it that much.'

'Ahhh, and I also stopped by the Mercedes dealership and saw the 2001 models. I saw one I really liked. I spoke with the salesman, and he gave me a really good price. And since we need to exchange the BMW that we bought last year...'

'What price did he quote you?'

'Only £45,000...'

'OK, but for that price I want it with all the options.'

'Great! But before we hang up, something else...'

'What?'

'It might look like a lot, but I was reconciling your bank account and I stopped by the estate agent this morning and saw the house we had looked at last year. It's on sale! Remember? The one with the pool and acre of land by the sea?'

'How much are they asking?'

'Only £460,000 – an amazing price… And we seem to have enough in the bank to cover…'

'Well, then go ahead and buy it, but just bid £440,000 – OK?'

'OK, love… Thanks! I'll see you later. I love you!'

'Bye… I do too…'

The man hangs up, closes the phone, raises his hand and asks all those present, 'Does anyone know who this phone belongs to?'

BATTLE OF THE SEXES

---— Original Message ———

From: webbo
To: willis
Sent: Monday, January 15, 2001 11:19 AM
Subject: FW: Men

Men are like... Laxatives. They irritate the shit out of you.

Men are like... Bananas. The older they get, the less firm they are.

Men are like... Holidays. They never seem to be long enough.

Men are like... Bank Machines. Once they withdraw, they lose interest.

Men are like... Weather. Nothing can be done to change either one of them.

Men are like... Blenders. You need one, but you're not quite sure why.

Men are like... Cement. After getting laid, they take a long time to get hard.

Men are like... Chocolate Bars. Sweet, smooth and they usually head right for your hips.

Men are like... Coffee. The best ones are rich, warm and can keep you up all night long.

Men are like... Commercials. You can't believe a word they say.

Men are like... Department stores. Their clothes should always be half off.

THE WORLD'S GREATEST EMAIL JOKE BOOK

Men are like… Government stocks. They take so long to mature.

Men are like… Horoscopes. They always tell you what to do and are usually wrong.

Men are like… Lawn mowers. If you're not pushing one around, then you're riding it.

Men are like… Mascara. They usually run at the first sign of emotion.

Men are like… Popcorn. They satisfy you, but only for a little while.

Men are like… Snowstorms. You never know when he's coming, how many inches you'll get or how long he'll last.

BATTLE OF THE SEXES

---------- Original Message ----------

From: willis
To: webbo
Sent: Wednesday, February 07, 2001 12:51 PM
Subject: FW: Hazardous material information bulletin

Element: Woman
Symbol: Wo
Discoverer: Adam
Atomic mass: Accepted at 53.6kg, but known to range from 40 to 200kg.
Occurrences: Copious quantities in all urban areas.

Physical properties:
1. Surface usually covered with painted film.
2. Boils in moments, freezes for no known reason.
3. Melts if given special treatment.
4. Bitter if incorrectly used.
5. Found in various states, ranging from virgin metal to common ore.
6. Yields to pressure applied to correct places.

Chemical properties:
1. Has great affinity for gold, silver and many other precious substances.
2. Absorbs great quantities of expensive substances.
3. May explode spontaneously without prior warning and for no known reason.

THE WORLD'S GREATEST EMAIL JOKE BOOK

4. Insoluble in liquids, but activity increases greatly by saturation in alcohol.
5. Most powerful money-reducing agent known to man.

Common uses:
1. Highly ornamental, especially in sports cars.
2. Can be a great aid to relaxation.
3. Very effective cleaning agent.

Tests:
1. Pure specimen turns rosy pink when discovered in natural state.
2. Turns green when placed next to a better specimen.

Hazards:
1. Highly dangerous, except in experienced hands.
2. Illegal to possess more than one, although several specimens can be maintained in different locations, as long as they do not come into contact with one another.

```
┌─────────────────────────────────────────┐
│ ▢ ═══════  BATTLE OF THE SEXES  ═══  ▣ ▤ │
└─────────────────────────────────────────┘

─────────────── Original Message ───────────────

From: willis
To: webbo
Sent: Monday, February 12, 2001 6:36 PM
Subject: If it really was a man's world...

1. Breaking up would be a lot easier. A smack on the arse and a 'Cheers for the sex – now f**k off' would pretty much do it.
2. Birth control would come in ale or lager.
3. Valentine's Day would be moved to 29 February, so it would only occur in leap years.
4. On Mother's Day, you'd get the day off to go drinking.
5. Instead of 'beer belly', you'd get 'beer biceps'.
6. Tanks would be far easier to rent.
7. Every woman that worked would have to do so topless.
8. Every man would get four real Get Out of Jail Free cards per year.
9. Telephones would cut off after 30 seconds of conversation.
10. When your girlfriend really needed to talk to you during the game, she'd appear in a little box in the corner of the screen when the ball goes out of play.
11. Nodding and looking at your watch would be deemed as an acceptable response to 'I love you.'
12. The funniest guy in the office would get to be CEO.
13. 'Sorry, but I got wasted last night' would be an
```

acceptable excuse for absence and/or poor time keeping.
14. Lifeguards could remove people from beaches for violating the 'public ugliness' ordinance.
15. Hallmark would make 'Sorry, what was your name again?' cards.
16. Lager would have the same effect as Viagra.
17. 'Fancy a shag?' would be the only chat-up line in existence and it would work every time.
18. Everyone would drive at least 145kph and anyone driving under that would be fined.
19. Dinner break would happen every hour and the boss would hire in strippers and £2,000-a-night hookers for the duration of those breaks.
20. Saying, 'Let's have a threesome. You, me and your sister' to your wife/girlfriend would get the response, 'What a great idea!!'
21. Harrier jump jets would take you to and from work.
22. Everyone would have a real light sabre and any disagreements would be settled by a fight to the death.
23. Vomiting after 20 pints would actually make you more attractive to the opposite sex.
24. When it was time to leave work, a whistle would sound and you'd get to slide down the back of a brontosaurus like Fred Flintstone.

BATTLE OF THE SEXES

---— Original Message ———

From: webbo
To: willis
Sent: Thursday, November 13, 2003 5:00 PM
Subject: FW: Five kinds of sex

Recent research shows that there are five kinds of sex:

The first kind of sex is Smurf Sex. This kind of sex happens when you first meet someone and you both have sex until you are blue in the face.

The second kind of sex is Kitchen Sex. This is when you have been with your partner for a short time and you are so horny you will have sex anywhere, even in the kitchen.

The third kind of sex is Bedroom Sex. This is when you have been with your partner for a long time. Your sex has become routine and you usually have sex in your bedroom.

The fourth kind of sex is Hallway Sex. This is when you have been with your partner for too long. When you pass each other in the hallway you both say, 'F**k you!'

The fifth kind of sex is Courtroom Sex. This is when you cannot stand your wife any more. She takes you to court and screws you in front of everyone.

THE WORLD'S GREATEST EMAIL JOKE BOOK

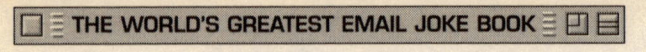

——————— Original Message ———————

From: webbo
To: willis
Sent: Tuesday, October 28, 2003 7:18 PM
Subject: FW: Dear Diary...

Here is a little story that we men could learn something from:

Dear Diary,

I never quite figured out why the sexual urges of men and women differ so much. And I have never figured out the whole Venus and Mars thing. I have never figured out why men think with their head and women with their heart. I have never figured out why the sexual desire gene gets thrown into a state of turmoil when it hears the words 'I do'.

One evening last week, my wife and I were getting into bed. Well, the passion started to heat up, and she eventually said, 'I don't feel like it, I just want you to hold me.' I said, 'WHAT??!!' So she said the words that every husband on the planet dreads to hear: 'You mustn't be in tune with my emotional needs as a woman.' I'm thinking, 'What was her first clue?' I finally realised that nothing was going to happen that night so I went to sleep.

BATTLE OF THE SEXES

The very next day, we went shopping at a big department store. I walked around with her while she tried on three different, very expensive outfits. She couldn't decide which one to take, so I told her to take all three. She wanted matching shoes, so I said, 'Let's get a pair for each outfit.' Then we went to the jewellery department, where she got a pair of diamond earrings. Let me tell you, she was so excited. She must have thought I was one wave short of a shipwreck. I started to think she was testing me because she asked for a tennis bracelet when she doesn't even know how to play tennis. I think I knocked her for six when I said it was OK. She was almost sexually excited from all of this.

You should have seen her face when she said, 'I think this is all, dear. Let's go to the till.' I could hardly contain myself when I blurted out, 'No, darling, I don't feel like buying all of this stuff now.' You should have seen her face… It went completely blank. I then said, 'Really, darling! I just want you to HOLD this stuff for a while.' And just when she had this look like she was going to kill me, I added, 'You mustn't be in tune with my financial needs as a man.'

I suppose I won't be having sex again until sometime after the spring of 2008.

THE WORLD'S GREATEST EMAIL JOKE BOOK

──────── Original Message ────────

From: webbo
To: willis
Sent: Friday, April 06, 2001 12:34 PM
Subject: The brain transplant

In the hospital the relatives gathered in the waiting room, where their family member lay gravely ill. Finally, the doctor came in looking tired and sombre. 'I am afraid I am the bearer of bad news,' he said as he surveyed the worried faces. 'The only hope left for your loved one at this time is a brain transplant. It is an experimental procedure, semi-risky, and you will have to pay for the brain yourselves.' The family members sat silent as they absorbed the news. After a great length of time, someone asked, 'Well, how much does a brain cost?' The doctor quickly responded, 'Five thousand pounds for a male brain and £200 for a female brain.' The moment turned awkward. Men in the room tried not to smile, avoiding eye contact with the women, but someone actually smirked. A man, unable to control his curiosity, blurted out the question everyone wanted to ask. 'Why is the male brain so much more?' The doctor smiled at the childish innocence and so to the entire group said, 'It is just standard pricing procedure. We have to mark down the price of the female brains, because they have actually been used.'

BATTLE OF THE SEXES

— Original Message —

From: webbo
To: willis
Sent: Tuesday, March 09, 2004 6:46 PM
Subject: FW: Growing old

I phoned up a really gorgeous ex-girlfriend of mine the other day. We lost track of time, chatting about the wild nights we used to enjoy together. I couldn't BELIEVE it when she asked if I'd like to meet up and maybe rekindle a little of that magic.

'Wow!' I said. 'I don't know if I could keep pace with you now! I'm a bit older and a bit balder than when you last saw me!'

She giggled and said she was sure I'd meet the challenge!

'Yeah,' I said. 'Just so long as you don't mind a man with a waistband that's a few inches wider these days!'

She laughed and told me to stop being so silly! She teased me, saying she thought bald, tubby men were cute! 'Anyway,' she said, 'I've put on a couple of pounds myself!'

So I hung up.

THE WORLD'S GREATEST EMAIL JOKE BOOK

———————— Original Message ————————

From: webbo
To: willis
Sent: Tuesday, March 09, 2004 6:46 PM
Subject: FW: Bar jokes

Barman's revenge

A man walks into a bar one night and asks for a beer.
'Certainly, sir,' says the bartender. 'That'll be one pence.'
'One penny?!' exclaims the man.
'That's right,' says the bartender.
So the man glances at the menu and asks, 'Could I have a nice juicy T-bone steak, with chips, peas and a salad?'
'Certainly, sir,' replies the bartender, 'but all that comes to real money.'
'How much money?' the man enquires.
'Four pence,' he replies.
'Four pence?! Where's the person who owns this place?'
'Upstairs with my wife,' says the bartender.
'What's he doing with your wife?' asks the man.
'Same as what I'm doing to his business.'

Music

———————— Original Message ————————

```
From: webbo
To: willis
Sent: Tuesday, September 04, 2001 3:25 PM
Subject: FW: Out hunting
```

A drummer and bass player are out in the woods hunting when the bassist falls to the ground. He doesn't seem to be breathing and his eyes are rolled back in his head. The drummer whips out his mobile phone and calls 999. He gasps to the operator, 'My friend just keeled over. I think he's dead! What should I do?'

The operator, in a calm, soothing voice, says, 'Just stay calm. I can help. First, let's make sure he's dead.'

There is a silence, then a shot is heard. The drummer's voice comes back on the line. He says, 'OK, now what?'

THE WORLD'S GREATEST EMAIL JOKE BOOK

---— Original Message ———

From: willis
To: webbo
Sent: Tuesday, September 26, 2000 10:37 AM
Subject: FW: 'Sad' news

Sometimes we need to pause and remember what life is about...

There was a great loss, recently, in the entertainment world. Larry La Prise, the Detroit native who wrote the song 'The Hokey Cokey', died last week at age 93. It was especially difficult for the family to get him in the casket. They put his left leg in and ... well, things just started going downhill from there.

```
┌─────────────────── MUSIC ───────────────────┐
```

─────────── Original Message ───────────

From: willis
To: webbo
Sent: Sunday, September 03, 2000 12:07 AM
Subject: The blues

Here are some tips for any of you that are in pursuit of a career in the blues:

1. Most blues begin with 'Woke up this mornin'...' This is to differentiate blues musicians from most other musicians, who sleep past noon.

2. The nice thing about the blues is that, once you've written the first line, you're pretty much done with the second line too.

3. Chevys and Cadillacs are blues cars. Other acceptable blues modes of transportation are as follows:
a. Greyhound bus
b. Southbound train
c. Walkin'

4. Teenagers shouldn't sing the blues until they're old enough to get the electric chair if they shoot a man in Memphis.

5. You can have the blues in New York City, but not in

Vail (Colorado), or any town whose name ends in 'Beach'. St Louis, Chicago and Kansas City are other good towns for the blues.

6. Shot in the back by a jealous lover is a blues way to die. So is the electric chair. It is not a blues death if you die during liposuction treatment.

7. You have the right to sing the blues if:
a. you're blind;
b. you shot a man in Memphis;
c. you can't be satisfied.

8. But not if:
a. you shot an 85 at golf;
b. your dad left you a trust fund;
c. you once were blind but now can see.

9. Good places for the blues:
a. A highway
b. A jailhouse
c. An empty bed
d. A freight train

10. Bad places for the blues:
a. Yellowstone National Park (Wyoming and Montana)
b. The country club
c. Gallery openings
d. The Hamptons (Long Island, New York)

MUSIC

11. If you ask for water and your 'baby' gives you gasoline, that's the blues. Other blues drinks include:
a. wine;
b. whiskey;
c. muddy water.

12. Blues beverages do not include:
a. any drink with an umbrella;
b. any wine kosher for Passover;
c. Snapple (all flavours);
d. Jelly shots.

13. Picking a blues name:
a. Start with an infirmity (Blind, Li'l, Fat, Lame, Clubfoot).
b. Add Willie, Johnny or Joe.
c. Pick a US President (Washington, Johnson, Fillmore or Roosevelt).
d. Persons with names like Ashley, Chad, Kimberly, McKenzie, Brad or Tyler may not sing the blues, no matter how many men they shoot in Memphis.

➤ Politics

─────────── Original Message ───────────

```
From: webbo
To: willis
Sent: Wednesday, November 19, 2003 6:14 PM
Subject: FW: Queen and country
```

Tony Blair was at his weekly meeting with the Queen when he said, 'As I'm the PM, I'm thinking of changing how the country is referred to… I'm thinking that it should be a kingdom.' To which the Queen replied, 'I'm sorry, Mr Blair, but to be a kingdom, you have to have a king in charge – and you're not a king.'

Tony Blair thought a while and then said, 'How about a principality then?' To which the Queen replied, 'Sorry again, but to be a principality, you have to be a prince – and you're not a prince, Mr Blair.'

Again, Blair thought long and hard and came up with,

'How about an empire then?' The Queen, getting a little pissed off by now, replied, 'Sorry again, Mr Blair, but to be an empire you must have an emperor in charge – and you are not an emperor.'

Before Tony Blair could utter another word, the Queen said, 'I think we're doing quite nicely as a country!'

---————— Original Message ——————

From: willis
To: webbo
Sent: Friday, April 30, 2004 10:23 AM
Subject: FW: Bush tragedy

Washington:

A tragic fire on Wednesday destroyed the personal library of George W Bush. Both of his books have been lost. A spokesman said the president was devastated, as he had not finished colouring the second one. More details to come.

POLITICS

---— Original Message ———

From: webbo
To: willis
Sent: Wednesday, February 19, 2003 6:09 PM
Subject: FW: Very topical

Three Texas surgeons were having lunch together and discussing surgeries they had performed. One of them said, 'I'm the best surgeon in Texas. A concert pianist lost seven fingers in an accident. I reattached them and eight months later he performed a private concert for the Queen of England.'

One of the others said, 'That's nothing. A young man lost both arms and legs in a terrible accident. I reattached them and two years later he won two gold medals in field events in the Olympics.'

The third surgeon said, 'You guys are amateurs. Several years ago a guy who was high on cocaine and alcohol rode a horse head-on into a train travelling 130 kilometres per hour. All I had left to work with was the horse's ass and a cowboy hat. He's now president of the United States.'

🗆 ☰ THE WORLD'S GREATEST EMAIL JOKE BOOK ☰ 🗗 🗏

──────────── Original Message ────────────

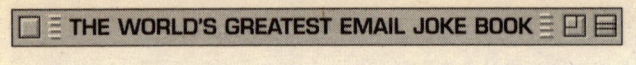

From: webbo
To: willis
Sent: Wednesday, November 01, 2000 11:47 AM
Subject: We're all in trouble...

Apparent utterings from the genius that is George W Bush:

'If we don't succeed, we run the risk of failure.'

'Republicans understand the importance of bondage between a mother and child.'

'Welcome to Mrs Bush, and my fellow astronauts.'

'Mars is essentially in the same orbit... Mars is somewhat the same distance from the Sun, which is very important. We have seen pictures where there are canals, we believe, and water. If there is water, that means there is oxygen. If oxygen, that means we can breathe.'

'The Holocaust was an obscene period in our nation's history. I mean in this century's history. But we all lived in this century. I didn't live in this century.'

'I have made good judgements in the past. I have made good judgements in the future.'

POLITICS

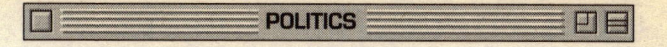

'I believe we are on an irreversible trend toward more freedom and democracy – but that could change.'

'One word sums up probably the responsibility of any governor, and that one word is "to be prepared".'

'Verbosity leads to unclear, inarticulate things.'

'The future will be better tomorrow.'

'We're going to have the best educated American people in the world.'

'People that are really very weird can get into sensitive positions and have a tremendous impact on history.'

'I stand by all the misstatements that I've made.'

'We have a firm commitment to NATO. We are a part of NATO. We have a firm commitment to Europe. We are a part of Europe.'

'Public speaking is very easy.'

'I am not part of the problem. I am a Republican.'

'A low voter turnout is an indication of fewer people going to the polls.'

'When I have been asked who caused the riots and the killing in LA, my answer has been direct and simple: Who is to blame for the riots? The rioters are to blame. Who is to blame for the killings? The killers are to blame.'

'Illegitimacy is something we should talk about in terms of not having it.'

'We are ready for any unforeseen event that may or may not occur.'

'For NASA, space is still a high priority.'

'Quite frankly, teachers are the only profession that teach our children.'

'The American people would not want to know of any misquotes that George Bush may or may not make.'

'We're all capable of mistakes, but I do not care to enlighten you on the mistakes we may or may not have made.'

'It isn't pollution that's harming the environment. It's the impurities in our air and water that are doing it.'

'[It's] time for the human race to enter the solar system.'

POLITICS

---------- Original Message ----------

From: webbo
To: willis
Sent: Saturday, November 25, 2000 3:10 PM
Subject: FW: 'Floriduh'

The truth, the mirror and the candidates...

Nader, Gore and Bush went to a fitness spa for some fun (if you believe Nader ever has fun) and relaxation (if you believe Gore ever relaxes). After a healthy lunch, all three decided to visit the men's room and found a strange-looking gent sitting at the entrance, who said, 'Welcome to the gentlemen's room. Be sure to check out our latest feature: a mirror that, if you look into it and say something truthful, will reward you with a wish. But be warned – if you say something false, you'll be sucked into the mirror to live in a void of nothingness for all eternity.'

They entered and, on finding the mirror, Nader said, 'I think I'm the most truthful of us three.' In an instant he was surrounded by a pile of money, which I suppose he invested in tech stocks.

Gore stepped up and said, 'I think I'm the most ambitious of us three.' And he suddenly found the keys to a new Lexus in his hand, which he liked because it looked better than the Veep's car.

Excited over the possibility of having a wish come true, Bush looked in the mirror and said, 'I think -' and was promptly sucked into the void.

─────────────── Original Message ───────────────

From: webbo
To: willis
Sent: Sunday, January 14, 2001 4:08 PM
Subject: Bush and Gore

Al Gore and George W Bush are having brunch at a diner. The attractive waitress asks Gore what he would like and he replies, 'I'll have a bowl of oatmeal and some fruit.'
'And what can I get for you, sir?' she asks George W. He replies, 'How about a quickie?'
'Why, Governor!' the waitress says. 'How rude — and you're not even a president yet!'
As she storms away, Gore leans over to Bush and whispers, 'It's pronounced "quiche".'

POLITICS

---------- Original Message ----------

From: willis
To: webbo
Sent: Friday, February 16, 2001 12:22 PM
Subject: FW: Clinton goes to Hell

Bill Clinton dies and is on his way to Hell. At Hell's gates he meets Satan. Satan tells Clinton that Hell is full, but that Clinton will be replacing one of the current inhabitants. Clinton will be given the choice of whom he will replace for ever in Hell.

Three doors appear before Clinton. The first door opens. Behind it is Newt Gingrich. He's being forced to pound big rocks into little rocks. Upon seeing Newt in this predicament, Clinton cringes and says, 'That looks painful. I don't think this is for me!' The second door opens. Behind it is Ted Kennedy. He is bobbing for automobile parts in a large pool of dirty water. Grimacing at the filthy scene, Clinton says, 'I don't think so.' The third door opens and behind it is Kenneth Starr. He's standing in his birthday suit with his hands on his hips. Kneeling before him is Monica Lewinsky, doing what she does best. 'I can handle that!' Clinton proclaims enthusiastically.

'Very well,' says Satan. 'Monica, you may go.'

THE WORLD'S GREATEST EMAIL JOKE BOOK

———————— Original Message ————————

From: webbo
To: willis
Sent: Saturday, January 03, 2004 2:28 PM
Subject: FW: Bush at the Pearly Gates

While walking down the street one day, George 'Dubya' Bush is shot and killed by a disgruntled National Rifle Association member. His soul arrives in heaven, and he is met by St Peter at the Pearly Gates. 'Welcome to Heaven,' says St Pete. 'Before you settle in, it seems there is a problem: We seldom know what to do with Republicans in these parts, and the same goes for you.'
'No problem, just let me in – I'm a believer,' says Dubya. St Pete shakes his head. 'I'd like to just let you in, but I have orders from the Man himself. He says you have to spend one day in Hell and one day in Heaven. Then you must choose where you'll live for eternity.'
'But, I've already made up my mind,' cries Dubya. 'I want to be in Heaven.'
'I'm sorry, but we have our rules,' St Pete says. And with that, Pete escorts Dubya to an elevator and he goes down, down, down, all the way to Hell.

The doors open, and Dubya finds himself in the middle of a lush golf course – the sun is shining in a cloudless sky, the temperature a perfect 72 degrees. In the distance is a beautiful clubhouse. Standing in front of it is his dad and thousands of other Republicans who had

POLITICS

helped him out over the years – people like Karl Rove, Dick Cheney and Jerry Falwell. Everyone is laughing and casually but expensively dressed. They run to greet Dubya, hug him and reminisce about the good times they had getting rich at expense of the 'suckers and peasants'. They play a friendly game of golf and then dine on lobster and caviar. The Devil himself comes up to Dubya with a frosty drink. 'Have a Margarita and relax, Dubya!'

'Uh, I can't drink no more, I took a pledge,' says Junior dejectedly.

The Devil laughs. 'This is Hell, son: you can drink and eat all you want and not worry, and it just gets better from there!'

Dubya takes the drink and finds himself liking the Devil, who he thinks is a really very friendly guy who tells funny jokes and pulls hilarious nasty pranks – a bit like a Yale Skull and Bones brother with real horns. They are having such a great time that, before he realises it, it's time to go. Everyone gives him a big hug and waves as Dubya steps on the elevator and heads upwards.

When the elevator door reopens, Dubya is in Heaven again and St Pete is waiting for him. 'Now it's time to visit Heaven,' the old man says, opening the gate. So, for 24 hours Bush is made to hang out with a bunch of honest, good-natured people who enjoy each other's company, talk about things other than money, and treat each other decently. Not a nasty prank or fraternity boy joke among them; no fancy country clubs and, while the food tastes great, it's not caviar or lobster. These people are all middle-class; he doesn't see anybody he knows; and he isn't even treated like someone special! Worst of all, to Dubya, Jesus turns out to be some kind of Jewish hippie with his endless 'peace' and 'do unto others' talk. 'Whoa,' Dubya says uncomfortably to himself, 'Pat Robertson never prepared me for this!'

The day done, St Peter returns and says to Dubya, 'Well, then, you've spent a day in Hell and a day in Heaven. Now choose where you want to live for eternity.'
With the 'Jeopardy' theme playing softly in the background, Dubya reflects for a minute, then answers, 'Well, I would never have thought I'd say this – I mean, Heaven has been delightful and all, but I really think I belong in Hell with my friends.' So Pete escorts Dubya to the elevator and he goes down, down, down, all the way to Hell.

The doors of the elevator open, and he is in the middle of a barren scorched earth covered with rubbish and toxic industrial waste – a bit like Houston. He is horrified to see all of his friends dressed in rags and chained together, picking up the rubbish and putting it in black bags. They are groaning and moaning in pain, faces and hands black with grime. The Devil comes over to Dubya and puts an arm around his shoulder. 'I don't understand,' says a shocked Dubya. 'Yesterday I was here and there was a golf course and a clubhouse, and we drank and ate caviar... I drank booze. We screwed around and had a great time. Now there's just a wasteland full of garbage, and everybody looks miserable.'

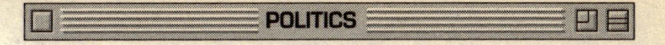

The Devil looks at Dubya and smiles slyly.'Yesterday we were campaigning; today you voted for us.'

🔥 Blondes

———————— Original Message ————————

```
From: willis
To: webbo
Sent: Tuesday, October 21, 2003 1:21 PM
Subject: FW: Blonde joke
```

A girl came skipping home from school one day. 'Mummy, Mummy,' she yelled, 'we were counting today, and all the other children could only count to four, but I counted to 10. See? 1, 2, 3, 4, 5, 6, 7, 8, 9, 10!'
'Very good,' said her mother.
'Is it because I'm blonde?' the girl asked.
'Yes, it's because you're blonde.'
The next day the girl came skipping home from school. 'Mummy, Mummy,' she yelled, 'we were saying the alphabet today, and all the other children could only say it to D, but I said it to G. See? A, B, C, D, E, F, G!'
'Very good,' said her mother.
'Is it because I'm blonde, Mummy?'

'Yes, it's because you're blonde.'

The next day the girl came skipping home from school. 'Mummy, Mummy,' she yelled, 'we were in gym class today and, when we showered, all the other girls had flat chests, but I have these!' And she lifted her tank top to reveal a pair of 36Cs.

'Very good,' said her embarrassed mother.

'Is it because I'm blonde, Mummy?'

'No, dear, it's because you're 24.'

——————————— Original Message ———————————

From: webbo
To: willis
Sent: Friday, April 06, 2001 12:34 PM
Subject: FW: Computer puzzle

A blonde girl enters a store that sells curtains. 'I'd like to buy a pink curtain that fits the size of my computer screen,' she tells the salesman.

The surprised salesman replies, 'But, madam, computers do not have curtains…'

'Helloooo…' says the blonde. 'I've got Windows!!!'

BLONDES

───────── Original Message ─────────

From: willis
To: webbo
Sent: Thursday, October 05, 2000 2:26 PM
Subject: Thursday joke

Two friends, a blonde and a redhead, are walking down the street and pass a flower shop, where the redhead happens to see her boyfriend buying flowers. She sighs and says, 'Oh, heck, my boyfriend is buying me flowers again … for no reason.'

The blonde looks quizzically at her and says, 'What's the problem – don't you like getting flowers?'

'Course I do,' says the redhead. 'But he always has expectations after giving me flowers, and I just don't feel like spending the next three days on my back with my legs in the air.'

'Don't you have a vase?' asks the blonde.

THE WORLD'S GREATEST EMAIL JOKE BOOK

---------- Original Message ----------

From: webbo
To: willis
Sent: Tuesday, January 14, 2003 7:21 PM
Subject: FW: Essex girl jokes

An Essex girl walks into the local dry cleaners. She places a garment on the counter. 'I'll be back tomorrow afternoon to pick up my dress,' she says.
'Come again?' says the assistant, cupping his ear.
'No,' she replies. 'This time it's mayonnaise.'

An Essex girl enters a sex shop and asks for a vibrator.
'Choose from our range on the wall,' says the man.
'I'll take the red one,' she says.
'That's a fire extinguisher,' the man replies.

An Essex girl is involved in a nasty car crash and is trapped and bleeding. The paramedics soon arrive on site.
Medic: 'It's OK I'm a paramedic and I'm going to ask you some questions?'
Girl: 'OK?'
Medic: 'What's your name?'
Girl: 'Sharon.'
Medic: 'OK, Sharon, is this your car?'
Sharon: 'Yes.'
Medic: 'Where are you bleeding from?'
Sharon: 'Romford, mate.'

BLONDES

An Essex girl was driving down the A13 when her car phone rang. It was her boyfriend, urgently warning her, 'Treacle, I just heard on the news that there's a car going the wrong way on the A13. Please be careful!'

'It's not just one car!' said the girl. 'There's hundreds of them!'

An Essex girl calls her boyfriend and says, 'Please come over and help me. I have a killer jigsaw puzzle, and I can't figure out how to get it started.'
'What is it supposed to be when it's finished?' asks her boyfriend.
'According to the picture on the box, it's a tiger,' she replies.
Her boyfriend decides to go and help with the puzzle. When he arrives she shows him where she has the puzzles spread all over the table. He studies the pieces for a moment, then looks at the box, then turns to her and says, 'First of all, no matter what we do, we're not going to be able to assemble these pieces into anything resembling a tiger. Second, I'd advise you to relax. Let's have a cup of coffee, then put all these Frosties back in the box.'

THE WORLD'S GREATEST EMAIL JOKE BOOK

———————— Original Message ————————

From: willis
To: webbo
Sent: Thursday, October 17, 2002 10:37 PM
Subject: Sailor

A depressed young woman was so desperate that she decided to end her life by throwing herself into the sea. When she went down the docks, a handsome young sailor noticed her tears and took pity on her. 'Look, you've got a lot to live for,' he said. 'I'm off to America in the morning, and if you like I can stow you away on my ship. I'll take good care of you and bring you food every day.' Moving closer, he slipped his arm around her shoulder and added, 'I'll keep you happy, and you'll keep me happy.' He winked. The girl nodded. After all, what did she have to lose? That night, the sailor brought her aboard and hid her in a lifeboat. From then on, every night he brought her three sandwiches and a piece of fruit and they made passionate love until dawn.

Three weeks later, during a routine search, the captain discovered her. 'What are you doing here?' he asked.
'I have an arrangement with one of the sailors,' she explained. 'He's taking me to America, and he's feeding me.'
'What are you doing for him?' said the captain.
'He's screwing me,' said the girl.
'He certainly is,' replied the captain. 'This is the Isle of Wight ferry.'

| BLONDES |

──────── Original Message ────────

From: willis
To: webbo
Sent: Wednesday, February 06, 2002 2:20 PM
Subject: FW: Space shuttle

A space shuttle mission is on its way to the moon with two monkeys and a woman on board. The US headquarters calls: 'Monkey number one, monkey number one to the television screen.' He sits down and he is told to release the pressure in compartment one, to increase the temperature in engine four, and to release oxygen to the reactors. The monkey promptly carries out his orders.

A few moments later, headquarters calls again: 'Monkey number two, monkey number two to the television screen.' He sits down and he is told to add carbon dioxide to room four, to stop the fuel injection to engine three, to add nitrogen to the fuel compartment, and to analyse the solar radiation. So monkey two does as he was asked.

A little later, headquarters calls again: 'Woman, please. Woman, approach the screen.' She sits down and, just as she is about to be told what to do, she says, 'I know, I know! Feed the monkeys and don't touch anything.'

THE WORLD'S GREATEST EMAIL JOKE BOOK

---------- Original Message ----------

From: willis
To: webbo
Sent: Friday, July 21, 2000 4:09 PM
Subject: FW: Perfume

Two blondes walk into a department store. They go up to the perfume counter and pick up a sample bottle. Sharon sprays it on her wrist and smells it. 'That's quite nice, innit, don't you fink, Trace?'
'Yeah, what's it called?'
'Viens à moi.'
'VIENS A MOI – what the does that mean?'
At this stage the assistant offers some help. "Viens à moi, ladies, is French for 'Come to me.'"
Sharon takes anther sniff and offers her arm to Tracey again, saying, 'That doesn't smell like come to me. Does that smell like come to you?'

BLONDES

—————— Original Message ——————

From: webbo
To: willis
Sent: Friday, August 04, 2000 3:33 PM
Subject: Ventriloquist

A ventriloquist is touring the clubs and stops to entertain in a small town. He's going through his usual 'dumb blonde' jokes when a well-presented blonde woman in the fourth row stands up and says, 'I've heard just about enough of your stupid blonde jokes! What makes you think you can stereotype women that way? What connection can a person's hair colour possibly have with their fundamental worth as a human being? It is morons like you that prevent women like myself from being respected at work and in our communities, and from reaching our full potential ... because you and your anachronistic kind continue to perpetuate negative images against not only blondes, but also women in general, for the sake of cheap laughs. You are a pathetic relic of the past, and what you do is not only contrary to discrimination laws in every civilised country, it is deeply offensive to people with modern sensibilities and basic respect for their fellow citizens. You should hang your head in shame, you pusillanimous little maggot.'

Flustered, the ventriloquist begins to apologise, when the blonde yells, 'You stay out of this, mister! I'm talking to that little bastard on your knee!'

THE WORLD'S GREATEST EMAIL JOKE BOOK

---------- Original Message ----------

From: willis
To: webbo
Sent: Friday, August 18, 2000 9:15 AM
Subject: Blind man's joke

A blind man on a barstool shouts to the bartender, 'Hey! Wanna hear a blonde joke?'

The bar immediately becomes absolutely quiet. In a hushed voice, the man next to him says, 'Before you tell that joke, you should know something. The bartender is blond, the bouncer is blond, and I'm a 1 metre 80 tall, 90kg blond with a black belt in karate. What's more, the guy sitting next to me is 1 m 85, weighs 100kg and he's a blond weightlifter,' he continues. 'The fella to your right is blond, 1 metre 92, pushing 135kg, and he's a wrestler. Think about it seriously, mister. You still wanna tell that joke?'

'Nah!' says the blind man. 'Not if I'm gonna have to explain it five times.'

BLONDES

———————— Original Message ————————

From: webbo
To: willis
Sent: Monday, May 17, 2004 10:26 PM
Subject: Casino

One night, two bored casino dealers were waiting at the crap table. A very attractive blonde woman arrived and bet £10,000 on a single roll of the dice. She said, 'I hope you don't mind, but I feel much luckier when I'm completely nude.' With that, she stripped from the neck down, rolled the dice and yelled, 'Come on, baby, Mama needs new clothes!' As the dice came to a stop she jumped up and down and squealed, 'YES! YES! I WON, I WON!' She hugged each of the dealers, then picked up her winnings and her clothes, and quickly departed. The dealers stared at each other dumbfounded. Finally, one of them asked, 'What did she roll?' The other answered, 'I don't know – I thought you were watching.'

Moral of the story: Not all blondes are dumb, but all men are men.

➔ Health

――――― Original Message ―――――

From: willis
To: webbo
Sent: Wednesday, December 06, 2000 11:16 AM
Subject: FW: Final countdown

A man hasn't been feeling well, so he goes to his doctor for a complete check-up. Afterwards, the doctor comes out with the results. 'I'm afraid I have some very bad news,' he says. 'You're dying, and you don't have much time left.'
'Oh, that's terrible!' says the man. 'How long have I got?'
'Ten,' the doctor says sadly.
'Ten?' the man asks. 'Ten what? Months? Weeks? What?!'
'Nine…'

THE WORLD'S GREATEST EMAIL JOKE BOOK

---— Original Message ———

From: webbo
To: willis
Sent: Thursday, February 13, 2003 8:43 PM
Subject: FW: New blood transfusion study

Today the American Medical Association announced that some patients needing blood transfusions may benefit from receiving chicken blood rather than human blood. Research reveals it tends to make the men cocky and the women lay better.

HEALTH

———————— Original Message ————————

From: webbo
To: willis
Sent: Tuesday, January 02, 2001 4:21 PM
Subject: Mix-up

Mr Smith went to the doctor's to collect his wife's test results:

Receptionist: 'I'm sorry, sir, but there has been a bit of a mix-up and we have a problem. When we sent your wife's sample to the lab, the sample from another Mrs Smith were sent as well, and we are now uncertain which one is your wife's. Frankly, that's either bad or terrible.'

Mr Smith: 'What do you mean?'

Receptionist: 'Well, one Mrs Smith has tested positive for Alzheimer's disease and the other for AIDS.'

Mr Smith: 'That's terrible! What am I supposed to do now?'

Receptionist: 'The doctor recommends that you drop your wife off in the middle of town and, if she finds her way home, don't shag her.'

THE WORLD'S GREATEST EMAIL JOKE BOOK

---------- Original Message ----------

From: webbo
To: willis
Sent: Wednesday, April 12, 2000 5:20 PM
Subject: FW: Poetry in motion

Tony Blair is being shown around a hospital. Towards the end of his visit, he is taken into a ward where there are a number of people with no obvious signs of injury. He goes to greet the first and the chap replies:
'FAIR fa' your honest sonsie face,
Great chieftain e' the puddin' race!
Aboon them a' ye tak your place,
Painch, tripe, or thairm:
Weel are ye wordy o' a grace,
As lang's my arm.'

Tony, being somewhat confused, goes to the next patient and greets him. He replies:
'Some hae meat, and canna eat,
And some wad eat that want it,
But we hae meat and we can eat,
And sae the Lord be thankit.'

Then the third patient rattles off:
'Wee sleekit, cow'rin, tim'rous beastie,
O, what a panic's in thy breastie!
Thou need na start awa sae hasty,
Wi bickering brattle!

HEALTH

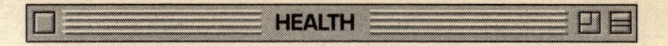

I wad be laith to rin an chase thee,
Wi murdering pattle!'

Tony turns to the doctor and asks what sort of ward this is — a mental ward?
'No,' replies the doctor. 'It's the Burns unit.'

THE WORLD'S GREATEST EMAIL JOKE BOOK

———————— Original Message ————————

From: webbo
To: willis
Sent: Wednesday, December 13, 2000 11:23 AM
Subject: Undesirable cures

Ending with a bang...

A man was having problems with premature ejaculation, so he decided to go to the doctor and ask what he could do to cure his problem.
'When you feel like you are getting ready to ejaculate, try startling yourself,' said the doctor.
That same day the man went to buy himself a starter pistol. All excited to try his doctor's suggestion, he ran home to his wife. There he found his wife in bed, naked and waiting. As the two began making love, they found themselves in the 69 position. Moments later, the man felt a sudden urge to ejaculate and fired the starter pistol.
The next day, the man went back to the doctor.
'How did it go?' asked the doctor.
'Not that well...' said the man. 'When I fired the pistol, my wife shit on my face, bit 8cm off my penis and my neighbour came out of the wardrobe with his hands in the air.'

HEALTH

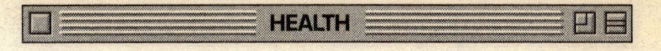

Help at a price...

One day a young man went into a pharmacy and asked the little old lady behind the counter if he could speak with the pharmacist.

'I am the pharmacist,' she informed him.

'Oh, in that case, forget it,' he replied and started to leave.

'Young man,' the lady said to him. 'My sister and I have been pharmacists for 40 years and there is nothing we haven't heard, so what is your problem?'

'Well,' the young man said reluctantly, 'I have a problem with erections. Once I get hard, it won't go down for hours and hours, no matter how much I masturbate or how many times I have intercourse! Please, can you give me something for it?'

'I'll have to go in the back and talk to my sister,' she replied. About ten minutes later she came back. 'Young man, I have consulted with my sister and the best we can give you is £300 a week and a third interest in the pharmacy.'

THE WORLD'S GREATEST EMAIL JOKE BOOK

---— Original Message ———

From: webbo
To: willis
Sent: Saturday, June 19, 2004 6:01 PM
Subject: FW: Doctor's surgery etiquette

An 86-year-old man walked into a crowded doctor's surgery. The receptionist said, 'Yes, sir, what are you seeing the doctor for today?'

'There's something wrong with my dick,' he replied.

The receptionist became irritated and said, 'You shouldn't come into a crowded surgery and say things like that.'

'Why not? You asked me what was wrong and I told you,' he said.

'You've obviously caused some embarrassment in this room full of people,' she replied. 'You should have said there is something wrong with your ear, or something, and then discussed the problem further with the doctor in private.'

'You shouldn't ask people things in a room full of others if the answer could embarrass anyone,' answered the man. He walked out, waited several minutes and then re-entered.

The receptionist smiled smugly and asked, 'Yes?'

'There's something wrong with my ear,' he stated.

The receptionist nodded approvingly and smiled, knowing he had taken her advice. 'And what is wrong with your ear, sir?'

'I can't piss out of it,' the man replied.

➤ Professional Life

---------- Original Message ----------

From: willis
To: webbo
Sent: Sunday, April 06, 2003 5:25 PM
Subject: FW: Two of a kind

A man walks into a bar and sees a good-looking, smartly dressed woman sitting on a barstool. He walks up behind her and says, 'Hi there, how's it going?'
Having already had a few drinks, she turns round to face him, looks him straight in the eyes and says, 'Listen! I'll screw anybody, any time, anywhere – your place, my place, it doesn't matter.'
'No kidding,' he says. 'I'm a lawyer too! What firm are you with?'

THE WORLD'S GREATEST EMAIL JOKE BOOK

---------- Original Message ----------

From: willis
To: webbo
Sent: Friday, August 25, 2000 4:47 PM
Subject: A legal misunderstanding

A Mafia godfather walks into a room, accompanied by his lawyer, to meet with his former accountant. 'Where's the three million bucks you embezzled from me?' the godfather asks the accountant. But the accountant does not answer.

The godfather asks again, 'Where's the three million bucks you embezzled from me?'

The lawyer interrupts, 'Sir, the man is a deaf mute and cannot understand you, but I can interpret for you.'

'Well, ask him where my damn money is!' says the godfather.

Using sign language, the lawyer asks the accountant the whereabouts of the three million dollars.

The accountant signs back, 'I don't know what you are talking about.'

The lawyer interprets this message to the godfather, who promptly pulls out a 9mm pistol, points it at the temple of the accountant, cocks the trigger and says, 'Ask him again where my damn money is!'

The lawyer signs to the accountant, 'He wants to know where it is!'

The accountant signs back. 'OK! OK! OK! The money

PROFESSIONAL LIFE

is hidden in a brown suitcase behind the shed in my back garden!'
'Well … what did he say?' says the godfather.
The lawyer interprets to him. 'He says … go to hell … you don't have the guts to pull the trigger.'

---------------- Original Message ----------------

From: willis
To: webbo
Sent: Friday, July 28, 2000 10:51 AM
Subject: The boss's revenge

After attending a party for his boss, the life and soul of the party was nursing a king-sized hangover and asked his wife, 'What the heck happened?'
'As usual, you made a fool of yourself in front of your boss,' replied the wife.
'Piss on him!' answered the husband.
'You did,' said the wife, 'and he fired you.'
'Well, screw him,' said the husband.
'I did, and you go back to work today.'

THE WORLD'S GREATEST EMAIL JOKE BOOK

Original Message

From: webbo
To: willis
Sent: Wednesday, March 26, 2003 10:55 AM
Subject: Who's boss?

One day all the body parts had a debate to decide who should be in charge of the body.

'I should be in charge,' said the blood, 'because I circulate oxygen all over, so without me you'd all waste away.'

'I should be in charge,' said the stomach, 'because I process food and give you all energy.'

'I should be in charge,' said the legs, 'because I carry the body wherever it needs to go.'

'I should be in charge,' said the eyes, 'because I enable the body to see where it goes.'

'I should be in charge' said the rectum, 'because I'm responsible for waste removal.'

All the other body parts laughed at the rectum and insulted him. So, in a huff, he shut down tight. Within a few days, the brain had a terrible headache, the stomach was bloated, the legs got wobbly, the eyes got watery and the blood was toxic. They all decided that the rectum should be the boss.

The moral of the story: The asshole is usually in charge.

PROFESSIONAL LIFE

———————— Original Message ————————

From: webbo
To: willis
Sent: Tuesday, March 20, 2001 3:04 PM
Subject: Business news from Japan

According to inside contacts, the Japanese banking crisis shows no signs of ameliorating. If anything, it's getting worse. Following last week's news that Origami Bank had folded, we are hearing that Sumo Bank has gone belly up and Bonsai Bank plans to cut back some of its branches. Karaoke Bank is up for sale and is (you guessed it!) going for a song. Meanwhile, shares in Kamikaze Bank have nose-dived and 500 back-office staff at Karate Bank got the chop. Analysts report that there is something fishy going on at Sushi Bank and staff there fear they may get a raw deal.

THE WORLD'S GREATEST EMAIL JOKE BOOK

---────── Original Message ──────---

From: willis
To: webbo
Sent: Friday, September 29, 2000 10:01 AM
Subject: FW: Lawyers' survival tactics

Two lawyers had been stranded on a deserted island for several months. The only other thing on the island was a tall coconut tree, which provided them with food. Each day the lawyers would take it in turns to climb to the top of the tree, to see if they could see a rescue boat.

One day, one of the men yelled down from the tree, 'Wow! I can't believe my eyes! I don't believe this is true!' His friend on the ground was sceptical and said, 'I think you're hallucinating and you should come down right now.'

So, the lawyer reluctantly climbed down the tree and told his friend he had just seen a naked blonde woman floating face up, and headed towards their island. The other lawyer started to laugh, thinking his friend had surely lost his mind.

But within a few minutes a naked blonde woman floated up to the beach. She was face up and totally unconscious.

The two lawyers went over to her and one said to the other, 'You know, we've been on this island for months now without a woman. It's been a long time... Do you think we should, you know, screw her?'

PROFESSIONAL LIFE

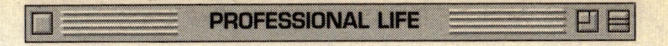

The other lawyer glanced down at the totally naked woman and asked, 'Out of what?'

THE WORLD'S GREATEST EMAIL JOKE BOOK

---——— Original Message ———---

From: willis
To: webbo
Sent: Monday, September 02, 2002 11:56 AM
Subject: FW: Business-growth advice

An investment banker was at the pier of a small coastal village when a small boat with just one fisherman docked. Inside the small boat were several large yellowfin tuna. The banker complimented the fisherman on the quality of his fish and asked how long it took to catch them.

'Only a little while,' replied the fisherman.

'So why don't you stay out longer and catch more fish?' said the banker.

'I have enough to support my family's immediate needs,' the fisherman explained.

The banker was curious. 'But what do you do with the rest of your time?'

'I sleep late, fish a little, play with my children, take a nap with my wife and each evening I stroll into the village, where I play guitar and sing with my friends,' said the fisherman. 'I have a full and busy life.'

The banker scoffed, 'I'm a Harvard MBA and I could help you. You should spend more time fishing and use the proceeds to buy a bigger boat. Then, with the proceeds from the bigger boat, you could buy several boats, and eventually you would have a fleet of fishing boats. Instead of selling your catch to a middleman, you

PROFESSIONAL LIFE

would sell directly to the processor, eventually opening your own cannery. You would control the product, processing and distribution. You would need to leave this small coastal fishing village and move to a big city, where you would run your expanding enterprise.'

'But how long would this all take?' asked the fisherman. To which the banker replied, 'Between 15 and 20 years.'

'But what then?'

The banker laughed. 'That's the best part,' he said. 'When the time is right, you would announce an Initial Public Offering, sell your company stock to the public and become very rich. You would make millions.'

'Millions... Then what?'

'Then you would retire,' said the banker. 'Move to a small coastal fishing village where you would sleep late, fish a little, play with your kids, take a nap with your wife and in the evenings stroll into the village, where you could play your guitar and sing with your friends.'

THE WORLD'S GREATEST EMAIL JOKE BOOK

―――――― Original Message ――――――

From: webbo
To: willis
Sent: Friday, July 05, 2002 7:47 AM
Subject: Poor performance

The following quotes were taken from actual employee-performance evaluations:

'Since my last report, this employee has reached rock bottom and has started to dig.'

'I would not allow this employee to breed.'

'This associate is really not so much of a has-been, but more of a definitely-won't-be.'

'This young lady has delusions of adequacy.'

'Works well when under constant supervision and cornered like a rat in a trap.'

'When she opens her mouth, it seems that this is only to change whichever foot was previously in there.'

'He sets low personal standards and then consistently fails to achieve them.'

'This employee is depriving a village of an idiot.'

'This employee should go far, and the sooner he starts the better.'

And these are actual quotes from military performance appraisals:

'Got into the gene pool while the lifeguard wasn't watching.'

'A room-temperature IQ.'

'Got a full six-pack, but lacks the plastic thingy to hold it all together.'

'A gross ignoramus – 144 times worse than an ordinary ignoramus.'

'A photographic memory but with the lens cover glued on.'

'Bright as Alaska in December.'

'Gates are down, the lights are flashing, but the train isn't coming.'

'He's so dense, light bends around him.'

'If he were any more stupid, he'd have to be watered twice a week.'

'It's hard to believe that he beat out 1,000,000 other sperm.'

PROFESSIONAL LIFE

———————— Original Message ————————

From: webbo
To: willis
Sent: Monday, April 22, 2002 5:36 PM
Subject: The bank letter

Dear Sir,

I am writing to thank you for bouncing the cheque with which I endeavoured to pay my plumber last month. By my calculations some three nanoseconds must have elapsed between his presenting the cheque and the arrival in my account of the funds needed to honour it. I refer, of course, to the automatic monthly deposit of my entire salary, an arrangement which, I admit, has only been in place for eight years.

You are to be commended for seizing that brief window of opportunity, and also for debiting my account with £30 by way of penalty for the inconvenience I caused to your bank. My thankfulness springs from the manner in which this incident has caused me to rethink my errant financial ways. You have set me on the path of fiscal righteousness. No more will our relationship be blighted by these unpleasant incidents in 2001, taking as my model the procedures, attitudes and conduct of your bank. I can think of no greater compliment, and I know you will be excited and proud to hear it. To this end, please be advised about the following changes:

I have noticed that, whereas I personally attend to your telephone calls and letters, when I try to contact you I am confronted by the impersonal, ever-changing, prerecorded, faceless entity that your bank has become. From now on, I, like you, choose only to deal with a flesh-and-blood person. Therefore my mortgage and loan repayments will hereafter no longer be automatic, but will arrive at your bank by cheque and be addressed personally and confidentially to an employee of your branch, whom you must nominate. You will be aware that it is an offence under the Postal Act for any other person to open such an envelope. Please find attached an Application for Authorised Contact Status, which I require your chosen employee to complete. I am sorry it runs to eight pages, but in order that I know as much about him or her as your bank knows about me, there is no alternative. Please note that all copies of his or her medical history must be countersigned by a Justice of the Peace, and that the mandatory details of his or her financial situation (income, debts, assets and liabilities) must be accompanied by documented proof. In due course I will issue your employee with a PIN number which he or she must quote in all dealings with me. I regret that it cannot be shorter than 28 digits but, again, I have modelled it on the number of button presses required to access my account balance via your telephone banking service.

As they say, imitation is the sincerest form of flattery. Let me level the playing field even further by

PROFESSIONAL LIFE

introducing you to my new telephone system, which, you will notice, is very much like yours. My Authorised Contact at your bank, the only person with whom I will have any dealings, may call me at any time and will be answered by an automated voice. Press the buttons as follows:

1) To make an appointment to see me.
2) To query a missing payment.
3) To transfer the call to my living room in case I am there.
4) To transfer the call to my bedroom in case I am sleeping.
5) To transfer the call to my toilet in case I am attending to nature.
6) To transfer the call to my mobile phone in case I am not at home.
7) To leave a message on my computer. (To leave a message, a password to access my computer is required. This password will be communicated to the Authorised Contact at a later date.)
8) To return to the main menu and listen carefully to options one to seven.
9) To make a general complaint or enquiry.

The Authorised Contact will then be put on hold, pending the attention of my automated answering service. While this may, on occasion, involve a lengthy wait, uplifting music will play for the duration. This month I've chosen a refrain from The Best of Woody Guthrie: 'Oh, the banks are made of marble, with a guard at every door, and the vaults are filled with silver, that the miners sweated for.' After 20 minutes of that, our mutual Contact will probably know it by heart.

On a more serious note, we come to the matter of cost. As your bank has often pointed out, the ongoing drive for greater efficiency comes at a cost, a cost that you have always been quick to pass on to me. Let me repay your kindness by passing some costs back. First, there is the matter of advertising material you send me. This I will read for a fee of £10 per page. Enquiries from your Authorised Contact will be billed at £3 per minute of my time spent in response. Any debits to my account – as, for example, in the matter of the penalty for the dishonoured cheque – will be passed back to you. My new phone service runs at 50p a minute (even Woody Guthrie doesn't come free of charge), so you would be well advised to keep your enquiries brief and to the point. Regrettably, but again following your example, I must also levy an establishment fee of 2% of my balance or £30 (whichever is more) to cover the setting up of this new arrangement.

May I wish you a happy, if ever-so-slightly less prosperous, New Year.

Your humble client
***

PROFESSIONAL LIFE

---------- Original Message ----------

From: willis
To: webbo
Sent: Wednesday, February 23, 2000 2:43 PM
Subject: Speaking out

The top 10 things you wish you could say at work:

1. I can see your point, but I still think you're full of shit.
2. I have plenty of talent and vision. I just don't give a f**k.
3. How about 'never'? Is 'never' good for you?
4. It sounds like English, but I can't understand a word you're saying.
5. I see you've set aside this special time to humiliate yourself in public.
6. Ah, I see the cock-up fairy has visited us again.
7. You are validating my inherent mistrust of strangers.
8. I'm already visualising the gaffer tape over your mouth.
9. Are you coming on to me or having a seizure?
10. The fact that no one understands you doesn't mean you're an artist.

Useful expressions for those high-stress days:

1. Well, aren't we just a ray of f**king sunshine?
2. Not the brightest crayon in the box now, are we?
3. Don't bother me. I'm living happily ever after.

THE WORLD'S GREATEST EMAIL JOKE BOOK

4. Do I look like a f**king people person?
5. This isn't an office. It's Hell with fluorescent lighting.
6. I pretend to work. They pretend to pay me.
7. You! Off my planet!!
8. Therapy is expensive; popping bubble wrap is cheap! You choose.
9. Practise random acts of intelligence and senseless acts of self-control.
10. I like cats too. Let's exchange recipes.
11. Did the aliens forget to remove your anal probe?
12. Errors have been made. Others will be blamed.
13. Let me show you how the guards used to do it.
14. And your cry-baby f**kwit opinion would be…?
15. I'm not crazy. I've just been in a very bad mood for 30 years.
16. Sarcasm is just one more service we offer.
17. Do they ever shut up on your planet?
18. I'm just working here till a good fast-food job opens up.
19. I'm trying to imagine you with a personality.
20. A cubicle is just a padded cell without a door.
21. Stress is when you wake up screaming and you realise you haven't fallen asleep yet.
22. I can't remember if I'm the good twin or the evil one.
23. How many times do I have to flush before you go away?
24. I just want revenge. Is that so wrong?
25. I work 40 hours a week to be this poor.

PROFESSIONAL LIFE

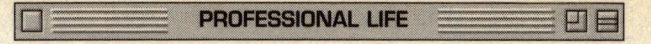

26. Can I trade this job for what's behind door number two?
27. Too many freaks; not enough circuses.
28. Just smile and say, 'Yes, mistress.'
29. Chaos, panic and disorder – my work here is done.
30. Earth is full. Go home.
31. Is it time for your medication or mine?
32. I plead contemporary insanity.
33. How do I set a laser printer to stun?
34. I'm not tense, just terribly, terribly alert.
35. When I want your opinion, I'll give it to you.

THE WORLD'S GREATEST EMAIL JOKE BOOK

---------- Original Message ----------

From: willis
To: webbo
Sent: Wednesday, March 15, 2000 12:06 PM
Subject: FW: Inspiring words...

The top 20 sayings you wish you could see on those office inspiration charts:

1. Rome did not create a great empire by having meetings; it did it by killing all those who opposed them.
2. If you can stay calm while all around you is chaos, then you probably haven't completely understood the seriousness of the situation.
3. Doing a job RIGHT the first time gets the job done. Doing the job WRONG 14 times gives you job security.
4. Eagles may soar, but weasels don't get sucked into jet engines.
5. Artificial Intelligence is no match for Natural Stupidity.
6. A person who smiles in the face of adversity probably has a scapegoat.
7. Plagiarism saves time.
8. If at first you don't succeed, try management.
9. Never put off until tomorrow what you can avoid altogether.

PROFESSIONAL LIFE

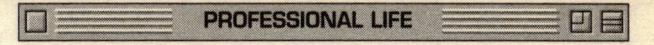

10. TEAMWORK means… never having to take all the blame yourself.
11. The beatings will continue until morale improves.
12. Never underestimate the power of very stupid people in large groups.
13. We waste time so you don't have to.
14. Hang in there, retirement is only 30 years away!
15. Go the extra mile. It makes your boss look like an incompetent slacker.
16. A snooze button is a poor substitute for no alarm clock at all.
17. When the going gets tough, the tough take a coffee break.
18. INDECISION is the key to FLEXIBILITY.
19. Succeed in spite of management.
20. Aim low, reach your goals, avoid disappointment.

THE WORLD'S GREATEST EMAIL JOKE BOOK

------ Original Message ---

From: willis
To: webbo
Sent: Wednesday, February 23, 2000 12:13 PM
Subject: An expanding business?

Imagine if major companies from all around the world started producing or sponsoring condoms. They would become fashionable and companies would probably advertise more openly…

Nike Condoms… Just do it.
Peugeot Condoms… The ride of your life.
Sony Condoms… Do not underestimate the power of Sony Condoms.
Microsoft Condoms… Where do you want to go today?
KFC Condoms… Finger-licking good.
M&Ms Condoms… Melt in your mouth, not in your hands.
Safeway Condoms… Lightening the load.
Abbey National Condoms… Because life's complicated enough.
Coca-Cola Condoms… The real thing.
Ever Ready Condoms… Keep going and going…
ESSO Condoms… The eye of the tiger.
Macintosh Condoms… It does more, it costs less, it's that simple.
Pringles Condoms… Once you pop, you can't stop.

PROFESSIONAL LIFE

Burger King Condoms... Home of the Whopper.
Goodyear Condoms... For a longer ride, go wide.
Vauxhall condoms... Raising the standard!
Philips Condoms... Let's make things better!
BT condoms... Stay in touch!
Halfords Condoms... We go the extra mile!
ONdigital condoms... Plug and play!

---— Original Message ———

From: willis
To: webbo
Sent: Monday, September 29, 2003 8:35 AM
Subject: Letter of resignation

Dear Mr Smith,

As an employee of an institution of higher education, I have a few very basic expectations. Chief among these is that my direct superiors have an intellect that ranges above the common ground squirrel. After your consistent and annoying harassment of my co-workers and myself during the commission of our duties, I can only surmise that you are one of the few true genetic wastes of our time.

Asking me, a network administrator, to explain every little nuance of everything I do each time you happen to stroll into my office is not only a waste of time, but also a waste of precious oxygen. I was hired because I know how to network computer systems, and you were apparently hired to provide amusement to myself and other employees, who watch you vainly attempt to understand the concept of 'cut and paste' for the hundredth time. You will never understand computers. Something as incredibly simple as binary still gives you too many options.

PROFESSIONAL LIFE

You will also never understand why people hate you, but I am going to try and explain it to you, even though I am sure this will be just as effective as telling you what an IP is. Your shiny new iMac has more personality than you ever will. You walk around the building all day, shiftlessly looking for fault in others. You have a sharply dressed, useless look about you that may have worked for your interview, but now that you actually have responsibility, you pawn it off on overworked staff, hoping their talent will cover for your glaring ineptitude. In a world of managerial evolution, you are the blue-green algae that everyone else eats and laughs at. Managers like you are sad proof of the Dilbert principle. Seeing as this situation is unlikely to change without you getting a full-frontal-lobotomy reversal, I am forced to tender my resignation. However, I have a few parting thoughts:

1. When someone calls you in reference to employment, it is illegal to give me a bad recommendation. The most you can say to hurt me is, 'I prefer not to comment.' I will have friends randomly call you over the next couple of years to keep you honest, because I know you would be unable to do it on your own.
2. I have all the passwords to every account on the system, and I know every password you have used for the last five years. If you decide to get cute, I am going to publish your 'favourites list', which I

conveniently saved when you made me 'back up' your useless files. I do believe that terms like 'Lolita' are not usually viewed favourably by the administration.

3. When you borrowed the digital camera to 'take pictures of your mother's birthday', you neglected to mention that you were going to take pictures of yourself in the mirror nude. Then you forgot to erase them, like the techno-moron you really are. Suffice it to say, I have never seen such odd acts with a ketchup bottle, but I assure you that those have been copied and kept in safe places pending the authoring of a glowing letter of recommendation. (Try to use a spellcheck, please. I hate having to correct your mistakes.)

Thank you for your time, and I expect the letter of recommendation on my desk by 8:00 a.m. tomorrow. One word of this to anybody and all of your little twisted repugnant obsessions will be open to the public. Never f*** with your systems administrator. Why? Because they know what you do with all that free time!

Sincerely,

PROFESSIONAL LIFE

———— Original Message ————

From: willis
To: webbo
Sent: Monday, September 29, 2003 10:45 AM
Subject: A job to be proud of

A primary-school teacher was asking her pupils what their parents did for a living.

'Tim, you be first,' she said. 'What does your mother do all day?'

Tim stood up and proudly said, 'She's a doctor.'

'That's wonderful. How about you, Amy?'

Amy shyly stood up, scuffed her feet and said, 'My father is a postman.'

'Thank you, Amy,' said the teacher. 'What about your father, Billy?'

Billy proudly stood up and announced, 'My daddy plays piano in a whorehouse.'

The teacher was aghast and promptly changed the subject to geography. Later that day she went to Billy's house and rang the bell. Billy's father answered the door. The teacher explained what his son had said and demanded an explanation. Billy's father said, 'I'm actually a lawyer. How can I explain a thing like that to a seven-year-old?'

THE WORLD'S GREATEST EMAIL JOKE BOOK

──────── Original Message ────────

From: willis
To: webbo
Sent: Wednesday, December 20, 2000 1:26 PM
Subject: Corporate Xmas card

Contract (& Legal) Dept seasonal greeting:
From us ('the wishor') to you (hereinafter called 'the wishee'). Please accept without obligation, implied or implicit, our best wishes for an environmentally conscious, socially responsible, politically correct, low-stress, non-addictive, gender-neutral celebration of the winter solstice holiday, practised within the most enjoyable traditions of the religious persuasion of your choice, or secular practices of your choice, with respect for the religious/secular persuasions and/or traditions of others, or their choice not to practise religious or secular traditions at all... And a financially successful, personally fulfilling and medically uncomplicated recognition of the onset of the generally accepted calendar year 2001, but with due respect for the calendars of choice of other cultures or sects, and having regard to the race, creed, colour, age, physical ability, religious faith, choice of computer platform or dietary preference of the wishee.

PROFESSIONAL LIFE

By accepting this greeting you are bound by these terms that:

* This greeting is subject to further clarification or withdrawal.
* This greeting is freely transferable provided that no alteration shall be made to the original greeting and that the proprietary rights of the wishor are acknowledged.
* This greeting implies no promise by the wishor to actually implement any of the wishes.
* This greeting may not be enforceable in certain jurisdictions and/or the restrictions herein may not be binding upon certain wishees in certain jurisdictions and is revocable at the sole discretion of the wishor.
* This greeting is warranted to perform as reasonably may be expected within the usual application of good tidings for a period of one year, or until the issuance of a subsequent holiday greeting, whichever comes first.
* The wishor warrants this greeting only for the limited replacement of this wish or issuance of a new wish at the sole discretion of the wishor.
* Any references in this greeting to 'the Lord', 'Father Christmas', 'Our Saviour', or any other festive figures, whether actual or fictitious, dead or alive, shall not imply any endorsement by or from them in respect of this greeting, and all proprietary rights in any referenced third-party names and images are hereby acknowledged.

🐾 Animals

──────────── Original Message ────────────

From: webbo
To: willis
Sent: Tuesday, March 25, 2003 12:16 AM
Subject: Talking dog

A man sees a sign outside a house saying: 'Talking dog for sale.' He rings the bell and the owner tells him the dog is in the garden. So the man goes into the garden and sees a black mutt just sitting there.
'You talk?' he asks.
'Yep,' the mutt replies.
'So, what's your story?'
The mutt looks up and says, 'Well, I discovered this gift when I was pretty young, and I wanted to help the government so I told MI6 about my gift. And in no time they had me jetting from country to country, sitting in rooms with spies and world leaders, because no one figured a dog would be eavesdropping. I was one of

their most valuable spies, eight years running. The jetting around really tired me out, and I knew I wasn't getting any younger and I wanted to settle down. So I signed up for a job at the airport to do some undercover security work, mostly wandering near suspicious characters and listening in. I uncovered some incredible dealings there and was awarded a batch of medals. Had a wife, a litter of puppies, and now I'm just retired.'

The man is astounded. He goes back in and asks the owner what he wants for the dog. 'Five pounds,' says the owner.

'But this dog is amazing,' says the man. 'Why on earth are you selling him so cheap?'

'He's such a f***ing liar. He didn't do any of that shit.'

ANIMALS

---- Original Message ----

From: willis
To: webbo
Sent: Friday, February 07, 2003 12:00 AM
Subject: Canine solution

A man was leaving a cafe with his morning coffee when he noticed a most unusual funeral procession approaching the nearby cemetery. A long black hearse was being followed by a second long black hearse about fifteen metres behind. Behind the second hearse was a solitary man walking a pit-bull dog on a leash. Behind him was a queue of 200 men walking in single file. Finally the man couldn't stand the curiosity. He respectfully approached the man walking the dog. 'I am so sorry for your loss, and I know now is a bad time to disturb you, but I've never seen a funeral like this. Whose funeral is it?'

'Well, that first hearse is for my wife,' the man replied.

'What happened to her?'

'My dog attacked and killed her,' he explained.

'Well, who is in the second hearse?'

'My mother-in-law,' said the man. 'She was trying to help my wife when the dog turned on her.'

A poignant and thoughtful moment of silence passed between the two men.

'Can I borrow the dog?'

'Join the queue.'

THE WORLD'S GREATEST EMAIL JOKE BOOK

---------- Original Message ----------

From: webbo
To: willis
Sent: Monday, October 30, 2000 3:02 PM
Subject: FW: Never have a talking parrot as a pet

A woman goes into a pet shop looking for a parrot. The assistant shows her a beautiful African grey parrot. 'What about this one, madam? A beautiful bird, I'm sure you'll agree, and it's an absolute steal at only £10.'

'Why is it so cheap?' the woman asks.

'Well,' replies the assistant, 'it used to live in a brothel and as a result its language is a touch fruity!'

'Oh, I don't mind that,' says the woman, making up her mind. 'I'm broad-minded and it'll be a laugh having a profane parrot.' So she buys the parrot and takes him home.

Once safely in his new home, the parrot looks around and squawks at the woman, 'F**k me, a new brothel and a new madam!'

'I'm not a madam and this isn't a brothel,' says the woman indignantly.

A little later the woman's two teenage daughters arrive home.

'A new brothel, a new madam, and now new prostitutes,' says the parrot when he sees the daughters.

'Mum, tell your parrot to shut up. We're not prostitutes,'

complain the girls, but they all see the funny side and have a laugh at their new pet.

A short while later, the woman's husband comes home. 'Well, f***k me, a new brothel, a new madam, new whores, but the same old clients. How ya doin', Dave?'

THE WORLD'S GREATEST EMAIL JOKE BOOK

---------- Original Message ----------

From: willis
To: webbo
Sent: Monday, December 11, 2000 11:26 AM
Subject: FW: The vet

A man brought a very limp dog into the veterinary clinic. As he laid the dog on the table, the vet pulled out his stethoscope, placing the receptor on the dog's chest. After a moment or two, the vet shook his head sadly and said, 'I'm sorry, but your dog has passed away.'

'What?' screamed the man. 'How can you tell? You haven't done any testing on him or anything. I want another opinion!' With that, the vet turned and left the room.

A few minutes later, he returned with a Labrador retriever. The retriever went right to work, thoroughly checking the poor dead dog with his nose. After a considerable amount of sniffing, the retriever sadly shook his head and said, 'Bark.' (Meaning: 'Dead as a doornail.')

The vet then took away the Labrador and returned with a cat, who also carefully sniffed the poor dog on the table. Like his predecessors, the cat sadly shook his head and said, 'Meow.' (Meaning: 'He's history.') He then jumped off the table and ran out of the room.

The vet handed the man a bill for £300. The dog's owner went berserk. 'Three hundred pounds just to tell me my dog is dead? This is outrageous!'

The vet shook his head sadly and explained. 'If you had

> **ANIMALS**

taken my word for it, the charge would have been £30, but with the lab work and the cat scan...'

──────────── Original Message ────────────

```
From: willis
To: webbo
Sent: Monday, June 21, 2004 10:20 PM
Subject: How to clean a cat
```

1. Thoroughly clean the toilet.
2. Lift both lids and add shampoo.
3. Find and soothe the cat as you carry him to the bathroom.
4. In one swift move, place the cat in the toilet, close both lids and stand on top so the cat cannot escape.
5. The cat will self-agitate and produce ample suds. (Ignore the ruckus from inside the toilet – the cat is enjoying this.)
6. Flush the toilet three or four times. This provides a power rinse, which is quite effective.
7. Have someone open the outside door, stand as far from the toilet as possible and quickly lift both lids.
8. The clean cat will rocket out of the toilet and outdoors, where he will air-dry.

Sincerely,
The Dog

⇨ Testing Times

---————— Original Message ——————---

From: willis
To: webbo
Sent: Friday, March 21, 2003 4:52 PM
Subject: FW: Embarrassing first date

This just tells you how hard it is to be single nowadays... This story was told on US TV series *The Tonight Show with Jay Leno*. Jay went into the audience to find the most embarrassing first date a woman ever had. The winner described her worst first-date experience and there was absolutely no question as to why her tale took the prize!

Marilyn said it was midwinter... snowing and quite cold... and the guy had taken her skiing to Lake Arrowhead, a mountain resort in southern California. It was a day trip (no overnight). Oh no, not Marilyn.

She was a good girl. They were strangers, after all, and had truly never met before.

The outing was fun but relatively uneventful until they were headed home late that afternoon. They were driving back down the mountain when Marilyn gradually began to realise that she shouldn't have had that extra latte. They were about an hour away from anywhere with a toilet and in the middle of nowhere! Her companion suggested she try to hold it, which she did for a while. Unfortunately, because of the heavy snow and slow going, there came a point when she told him that he had better stop and let her pee beside the road, or it would be the front seat of his car. They stopped and she quickly crawled out beside the car and yanked her pants down. Unfortunately, in the deep snow she didn't have good footing, so she let her backside rest against the rear mudguard to steady herself.

Her companion stood on the side of the car watching for traffic, and indeed was a real gentleman and refrained from peeking. All Marilyn could think about was the relief she felt, despite the rather embarrassing nature of the situation. Upon finishing, however, she soon became aware of another sensation. As she bent to pull up her pants, she discovered her buttocks were firmly glued against the car's mudguard. Thoughts of tongues frozen to pump handles immediately came to mind as she attempted to disengage her flesh from the

TESTING TIMES

icy metal. It was quickly apparent that she had a brand new problem due to the extreme cold. Horrified by her plight, and yet aware of the humour, she answered her date's concerns about 'what was taking so long' with a reply that she was 'freezing her butt off and needed some assistance!' He came round the car as she tried to cover herself with her sweater and then, as she looked imploringly into his eyes, he burst out laughing. She too got the giggles, and when they finally managed to compose themselves, they assessed her dilemma. Obviously, as hysterical as the situation was, they were also faced with a real problem. Both agreed it would take something hot to free her chilly cheeks from the grip of the icy metal!

Thinking about what had got her into the predicament in the first place, both quickly realised that there was only one way to get her free. So, as she looked the other way, her first-time date proceeded to unzip his pants and pee her backside off the mudguard.

As for *The Tonight Show*, she took the prize hands down — or perhaps that should be 'pants down'. And you thought your first date was embarrassing…

```
From: willis
To: webbo
Sent: Wednesday, April 24, 2002 11:37 PM
Subject: FW: The Queen Mother
```

Apparent excerpts from the Queen Mum's Book of Remembrance:

'When Diana died I swore I would never smile again, but eventually I did. Now the Queen Mum has gone I cannot imagine that I will ever smile for the rest of my life, but I will probably break that one too.'

'She was one of the old school. All the remaining royals are shit.'

'I thought she would never die, she has let us all down very badly.'

'She was a marvellous woman, and a wonderful lover.'

'I am absolutely devastated. At least we could have got the day off.'

'How refreshing to be able to mourn the death of a member of the royal family without being accused of being homosexual.'

TESTING TIMES

'Her death should act as a warning to others who think it is cool to experiment with drugs.'

'On behalf of all blacks, I send the sincerest condolences.'

'Perhaps if we automated her old golf buggy it could still drive around the Mall on its own and bring pleasure to the tourists.'

'Once again the Queen is not upset enough for my liking. The woman should have a bit more compassion. How would she feel if it were her mother?'

'It is such a loss. God has shat on our heads.'

'I am sure the Queen Mum will not let this small setback put an end to her public duties.'

'I hold Princess Margaret in no small way responsible for this terrible event.'

'We must do all we can – send blankets, food parcels, jumpers, anything – to help these brave souls who are queuing up to walk past her coffin.'

'I have been unable to masturbate for five days, and will not do so again until Her Majesty is buried.'

'Good God, who is next, Geri Halliwell?'
R Combes, Romford

'Whichever way you look at it, it just is not as exciting as Diana.'

'She was one of us, and by that I don't mean she perpetrated insurance fraud or lied about expense claims. She was like us in a good way. God bless you, ma'am.'

'If only I could get my hands on that fish bone right now, you heartless bastard!'

'She had such a difficult life, always battling against adversity and misfortune. Let us hope that, if there is a next time round, she is given a life of privilege and comfort.'

TESTING TIMES

---------- Original Message ----------

From: webbo
To: willis
Sent: Monday, February 26, 2001 11:24 AM
Subject: FW: Turning the tables

When I was younger I hated going to weddings. It seemed that all of my aunts and the grandmotherly types used to come up to me, poke me in the ribs, cackle and tell me, 'You're next.' They stopped that crap after I started doing the same thing to them at funerals.

---------- Original Message ----------

From: willis
To: webbo
Sent: Wednesday, November 01, 2000 6:25 PM
Subject: Silence in court

These are things people actually said in court, word for word, taken down and now published by court reporters who had the torment of staying calm during these exchanges:

Q: What is your date of birth?
A: 15 July.

THE WORLD'S GREATEST EMAIL JOKE BOOK

Q: What year?
A: Every year.

Q: What gear were you in at the moment of the impact?
A: Gucci sweats and Reeboks.

Q: This myasthenia gravis, does it affect your memory at all?
A: Yes.

Q: And in what ways does it affect your memory?
A: I forget.
Q: You forget. Can you give us an example of something that you've forgotten?

Q: How old is your son, the one living with you?
A: Thirty-eight or thirty-five, I can't remember which.

Q: How long has he lived with you?
A: Forty-five years.

Q: What was the first thing your husband said to you when he woke that morning?
A: He said, 'Where am I, Cathy?'
Q: And why did that upset you?
A: My name is Susan.

TESTING TIMES

Q: And where was the location of the accident?
A: Approximately milepost 499.
Q: And where is milepost 499?
A: Probably between milepost 498 and 500.

Q: Sir, what is your IQ?
A: Well, I can see pretty well, I think.

Q: Did you blow your horn or anything?
A: After the accident?
Q: Before the accident.
A: Sure, I played for 10 years. I even went to school for it.

Q: Do you know if your daughter has ever been involved in voodoo or the occult?
A: We both do.
Q: Voodoo?
A: We do.
Q: You do?
A: Yes, voodoo.

Q: Sergeant, when you stopped the defendant, were your blue lights flashing?
A: Yes.

THE WORLD'S GREATEST EMAIL JOKE BOOK

Q: Did the defendant say anything when she got out of her car?
A: Yes, sir.
Q: What did she say?
A: What disco am I at?

Q: Now, doctor, isn't it true that when a person dies in his sleep he doesn't know about it until the next morning?

Q: The youngest son, the 20-year old, how old is he?

Q: Were you present when your picture was taken?

Q: So the date of conception (of the baby) was 8 August?
A: Yes.
Q: And what were you doing at that time?
Q: She had three children, right?
A: Yes.
Q: How many were boys?
A: None.
Q: Were there any girls?

Q: You say the stairs went down to the basement?
A: Yes.
Q: And these stairs, did they go up also?

TESTING TIMES

Q: How was your first marriage terminated?
A: By death.
Q: And by whose death was it terminated?

Q: Can you describe the individual?
A: He was about medium height and had a beard.
Q: Was this a male or a female?

Q: Is your appearance here this morning pursuant to a deposition notice that I sent to your attorney?
A: No, this is how I dress when I go to work.

Q: Doctor, how many autopsies have you performed on dead people?
A: All my autopsies are performed on dead people.

Q: All your responses must be oral, OK? What school did you go to?
A: Oral.
Q: Do you recall the time that you examined the body?
A: The autopsy started around 8:30 p.m.
Q: And Mr Dennington was dead at the time?
A: No, he was sitting on the table wondering why I was doing an autopsy.

Q: Are you qualified to give a urine sample?

THE WORLD'S GREATEST EMAIL JOKE BOOK

---- Original Message ----

From: willis
To: webbo
Sent: Friday, November 10, 2000 11:19 AM
Subject: FW: $ubliminal college letter

Dear Dad,
$chool i$ really great. I am making lot$ of friend$ and $tudying very hard. With all my $tuff, I $imply can't think of anything I need. $o you can ju$t $end me a card, a$ I would love to hear from you.

Love,
Your $on

Dear Son,
I kNOw that astroNOmy, ecoNOmics and oceaNOgraphy are eNOugh to keep even an hoNOurs student busy. Do NOt forget that the pursuit of kNOwledge is a NOble task. You can never study eNOugh.

Love, Dad

TESTING TIMES

──────── Original Message ────────

From: willis
To: webbo
Sent: Thursday, December 21, 2000 6:07 PM
Subject: FW: Hangovers

1 star hangover
No pain. No real feeling of illness. Your sleep last night was a mere disco nap, which is giving you a whole lot of misplaced energy. Be glad that you are able to function relatively well. However, you are still parched. You can drink 10 bottles of water and still feel this way. Even vegetarians are craving a cheeseburger and a side of fries.

2 star hangover
No pain. Something is definitely amiss. You may look OK but you have the attention span and mental capacity of a stapler. The coffee you chug, to try and remain focused, is only exacerbating your rumbling gut, which is craving a full-on English breakfast. Last night has wreaked havoc on your bowels and, even though you have a nice demeanour about the office, you are costing your employer valuable money because all you really can handle is aimlessly surfing the Net and writing junk e-mails.

3 star hangover

Slight headache. Stomach feels crappy. You are definitely a space cadet and so not productive. Any time a girl walks by, you gag because her perfume reminds you of the random gin shots you had with your alcoholic friends after the bouncer kicked you out at 1:45 a.m. Life would be better right now if you were in your bed with a dozen doughnuts and a litre of Coke watching *This Morning* with Richard and Judy. You've had four cups of coffee, four litres of water, two sausage solls and a litre of Diet Coke – yet you haven't peed once.

4 star hangover

You have lost the will to live. Your head is throbbing and you can't speak too quickly or else you might honk. Your boss has already lambasted you for being late and has given you a lecture for reeking of booze. You wore nice clothes, but that can't hide the fact that you missed an oh-so crucial spot shaving (girls, it looks like you put your make-up on while riding the bumper cars), your teeth have sweaters, your eyes look like one big vein and your hairstyle makes you look like a reject from the class picture of Moss Side Secondary School circa 1976. You would give a week's pay for one of the following:
1. Home time.
2. A duvet and space to be alone.
3. A time machine so you could go back and NOT have gone out the night before.

TESTING TIMES

5 star hangover, aka Dante's Fourth Circle of Hell

You have a second heartbeat in your head, which is actually annoying the employee who sits next to you. Vodka vapour is seeping out of every pour and making you dizzy. You still have toothpaste crust in the corners of your mouth from brushing your teeth. Your body has lost the ability to generate saliva, so your tongue is suffocating you. You'd cry but that would take the last of the moisture left in your body. Death seems pretty good right now. Your boss doesn't even get mad at you and your co-workers think that your dog just died because you look so pathetic. You should have called in sick because, let's face it, all you can manage to do is breathe… very gently.

———————— Original Message ————————

From: webbo
To: willis
Sent: Monday, February 05, 2001 2:13 PM
Subject: FW: A few nice nursery rhymes

Mary had a little lamb.
Her father shot it dead.
Now it goes to school with her,
Between two hunks of bread.

Mary had a little lamb.
It ran into a pylon.
10,000 volts went up its ass
And turned its wool to nylon.

Little Miss Muffet sat on a tuffet,
Her clothes all tattered and torn.
It wasn't the spider that crept beside her,
But Little Boy Blue and his horn.

Simple Simon met a pieman, going to the fair.
Said Simple Simon to the pieman,
What have you got there?
Said the pieman unto Simon,
Pies, you dickhead.

Humpty Dumpty sat on a wall.
Humpty Dumpty had a great fall.
All the king's horses and all the king's men
Said, 'F**k him, he's only an egg.'

Georgie Porgy pudding and pie.
Kissed the girls and made them cry.
When the boys came out to play,
He kissed them too, 'cause he was gay.

TESTING TIMES

Jack and Jill
Went up the hill
To have a little fun.
Jill, that dill,
Forgot her Pill
And now they have a son.

Old Mother Hubbard
Went to the cupboard,
To fetch her poor dog a bone.
When she bent over,
Rover took over
And gave her a bone of his own.

Little Boy blew…
Hey. He needed the money.

THE WORLD'S GREATEST EMAIL JOKE BOOK

———————— Original Message ————————

From: webbo
To: willis
Sent: Friday, February 16, 2001 12:22 PM
Subject: FW: Quotes from the Montreal Comedy Festival

'You're basically killing each other to see who's got the better imaginary friend.' (On going to war over religion.)

'I found my wife in bed naked one day next to a Vietnamese guy and a black guy. I took a picture and sent it to Benetton. You never know.'

'I got kicked out of Riverdance for using my arms.'

'On the one hand, we'll never experience childbirth. On the other hand, we can open all our own jars.' (On the difference between men and women.)

'And God said: "Let there be Satan, so people don't blame everything on Me. And let there be lawyers, so people don't blame everything on Satan."'

'What are the three words guaranteed to humiliate men everywhere? "Hold my purse."'

'The Web brings people together because, no matter

TESTING TIMES

what kind of a twisted sexual mutant you happen to be, you've got millions of pals out there.'

'Type in "Find people that have sex with goats that are on fire" and the computer will say, "Specify type of goat."'

'Women might be able to fake orgasms, but men can fake whole relationships.'

'There are only two reasons to sit in the back row of a plane: either you have diarrhoea, or you're anxious to meet people who do.'

'My girlfriend always laughs during sex, no matter what she's reading.'

'My cousin just died. He was only 19. He got stung by a bee – the natural enemy of a tightrope walker.'

'I saw a woman wearing a sweatshirt with "Guess" on it. I said, "Thyroid problem?"'

'Honesty is the key to a relationship. If you can fake that, you're in.'

'Hockey is a sport for white men. Basketball is a sport

for black men. Golf is a sport for white men dressed like black pimps.'

'Things you'll never hear a woman say: "My, what an attractive scrotum!"'

'I read somewhere that 77% of all the mentally ill live in poverty. Actually, I'm more intrigued by the 23% who are apparently doing quite well for themselves.'

'My parents saw the president they loved get shot in the head. I saw my president get head.'

'I discovered I scream the same way whether I'm about to be devoured by a Great White or if a piece of seaweed touches my foot.'

'My mother never saw the irony in calling me a son of a bitch.'

TESTING TIMES

――――――――― Original Message ―――――――――

From: willis
To: webbo
Sent: Wednesday, January 14, 2004 10:37 AM
Subject: FW: Romantic rhymes

These are entries to a *Washington Post* competition asking for a rhyme with the most romantic first line... but the least romantic second line:

Love may be beautiful, love may be bliss;
But I slept with you only because I was pissed.

I thought that I could love no other.
Until, that is, I met your brother.

Roses are red, violets are blue, sugar is sweet, and so are you.
But the roses are wilting, the violets are dead, the sugar bowl's empty, and so is your head.

On loving beauty you float with grace.
If only you could hide your face!

Kind, intelligent, loving, and hot;
This describes everything you are not.

I want to feel your sweet embrace.
But don't take that paper bag off of your face.

THE WORLD'S GREATEST EMAIL JOKE BOOK

I love your smile, your face, and your eyes;
Damn, I'm good at telling lies!

My darling, my lover, my beautiful wife,
Marrying you screwed up my life.

I see your face when I am dreaming...
That's why I always wake up screaming.

My love, you take my breath away.
What have you stepped in to smell this way?

My feelings for you no words can tell,
Except for maybe 'Go to hell'!

What inspired this amorous rhyme?
Two parts vodka, one part lime.

TESTING TIMES

―――――― Original Message ――――――

From: webbo
To: willis
Sent: Monday, January 26, 2004 6:58 PM
Subject: FW: Alternative definitions

The *Washington Post* publishes a yearly contest in which readers are asked to supply alternative meanings for various words. These are the 2002 winners:

1. Coffee (n.), a person who is coughed upon.

2. Flabbergasted (adj.), appalled over how much weight you have gained.

3. Abdicate (v.), to give up all hope of ever having a flat stomach.

4. Esplanade (v.), to attempt an explanation while drunk.

5. Willy-nilly (adj.), impotent.

6. Negligent (adj.), describes a condition in which you absentmindedly answer the door in your nightgown.

7. Lymph (v.), to walk with a lisp.

8. Gargoyle (n.), an olive-flavoured mouthwash.

9. Flatulence (n.), the emergency vehicle that picks you up after you have been run over by a steamroller.

10. Balderdash (n.), a rapidly receding hairline.

11. Testicle (n.), a humorous question on an exam.

12. Rectitude (n.), the formal, dignified demeanour assumed by a proctologist immediately before he examines you.

13. Oyster (n.), a person who sprinkles his conversation with Yiddish expressions.

14. Circumvent (n.), the opening in the front of boxer shorts.

↪ Religion

---------- Original Message ----------

From: willis
To: webbo
Sent: Friday, May 21, 2004 1:32 PM
Subject: Confession

A housewife takes a lover during the day, while her husband is at work. But, unknown to her, her nine-year-old son is hiding in the wardrobe. When her husband comes home unexpectedly, she hides her lover in the wardrobe. Now the boy has company:

Boy: 'Dark in here.'
Man: 'Yes, it is.'
Boy: 'I have a cricket ball.'
Man: 'That's nice.'
Boy: 'Want to buy it?'
Man: 'No, thanks.'
Boy: 'My dad's outside.'

Man: 'OK, how much?'
Boy: '£100.'

A few weeks later, once again the boy and his mum's lover find themselves in the wardrobe together:

Boy: 'Dark in here.'
Man: 'Yes, it is.'
Boy: 'I have a cricket bat.'
Man: 'How much?'
Boy: '£400.'
Man: 'Fine.'

A few days later, the father says to the boy, 'Grab your cricket bat. Let's go outside and do a bit of practice.'
'I can't,' says the boy. 'I sold them.'
'How much did you sell them for?' the father asks.
'Five hundred pounds.'
'That's terrible to overcharge your friends like that,' says his father. 'That is way more than those two things cost. I'm going to take you to church and make you confess.'
So they go to church and the father alerts the priest, makes the little boy sit in the confession booth and closes the door.
'Dark in here,' says the boy.
'Don't start that shit again,' says the priest.

RELIGION

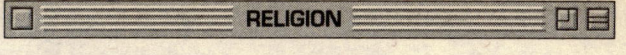

―――――― Original Message ――――――

From: willis
To: webbo
Sent: Tuesday, October 07, 2003 8:53 PM
Subject: Wedding night

An Irish Catholic lad goes up to his mother on the eve of his wedding night and asks, 'Mum, why are wedding dresses white?'

The mother looks at her son and replies, 'Son, this shows the town that your bride is pure.'

The son thanks his mum and goes off to double-check this with his father. 'Dad, why are wedding dresses white?'

The father sips his whiskey and looks at his son in surprise and says, 'Son, all household appliances come in white.'

THE WORLD'S GREATEST EMAIL JOKE BOOK

---------- Original Message ----------

From: webbo
To: willis
Sent: Saturday, February 24, 2001 12:38 PM
Subject: Prayers

Female prayer:

Before I lay me down to sleep,
I pray for a man who's not a creep,
One who's handsome, smart and strong,
One who loves to listen long,
One who thinks before he speaks,
One who'll call, not wait for weeks.
I pray he's gainfully employed,
So when I spend his cash he won't be annoyed,
I pray he pulls out my chair and opens my door,
Massages my back and begs to do more.
Oh! Send me a man who'll make love to my mind,
Knows what to answer to 'How big is my behind?'
I pray that this man will love me no end,
And never attempt to hit on my friend.
Amen.

Male prayer:

I pray for a deaf-mute nymphomaniac with perky boobs who owns an off-licence.

RELIGION

── Original Message ──

From: willis
To: webbo
Sent: Wednesday, August 16, 2000 2:20 PM
Subject: Why can't I own a Canadian?

For those of you that are not following the recent controversy surrounding Laura Schlessinger, she is a US radio talk-show host who dispenses ethical and moral advice to her callers. Paramount Television Group is also currently producing a Dr Laura TV show. Dr Laura is a recent convert to Judaism and is now Ba'al T'shuvah. Not long ago she made some statements about homosexuals that have caused the Canadian anti-hate laws to censure her. The following is an open letter to Dr Laura, which was posted on the Internet:

Dear Dr Laura,

Thank you for doing so much to educate people regarding God's Law. I have learned a great deal from your show, and I try to share that knowledge with as many people as I can. When someone tries to defend the homosexual lifestyle, for example, I simply remind him that Leviticus 18:22 clearly states it to be an abomination. End of debate.

I do need some advice from you, however, regarding some of the specific laws and how to best follow them:

THE WORLD'S GREATEST EMAIL JOKE BOOK

a) When I burn a bull on the altar as a sacrifice, I know it creates a pleasing odour for the Lord (Lev. 1:9). The problem is my neighbours. They claim the odour is not pleasing to them. Should I smite them?

b) I would like to sell my daughter into slavery, as sanctioned in Exodus 21:7. In this day and age, what do you think would be a fair price for her?

c) I know that I am allowed no contact with a woman while she is in her period of menstrual uncleanliness (Lev. 15:19 - 24). The problem is, how do I tell? I have tried asking, but most women take offence.

d) Lev. 25:44 states that I may indeed possess slaves, both male and female, provided they are purchased from neighbouring nations. A friend of mine claims that this applies to Mexicans, but not Canadians. Can you clarify? Why can't I own Canadians?

e) I have a neighbour who insists on working on the Sabbath. Exodus 35:2 clearly states he should be put to death. Am I morally obligated to kill him myself?

f) A friend of mine feels that, even though eating shellfish is an abomination (Lev. 11:10), it is a lesser abomination than homosexuality. I don't agree. Can you settle this?

g) Lev. 21:20 states that I may not approach the altar of God if I have a defect in my sight. I have to admit that I wear reading glasses. Does my vision have to be 20/20, or is there some wiggle room here?

h) Most of my male friends get their hair trimmed, including the hair around their temples, even though

RELIGION

this is expressly forbidden by Lev. 19:27. How should they die?

i) I know from Lev. 11:6 - 8 that touching the skin of a dead pig makes me unclean, but may I still play football if I wear gloves?

j) My uncle has a farm. He violates Lev. 19:19 by planting two different crops in the same field, as does his wife by wearing garments made of two different kinds of thread (cotton/polyester blend). He also tends to curse and blaspheme a lot. Is it really necessary that we go to all the trouble of getting the whole town together to stone them (Lev. 24:10 - 16)? Couldn't we just burn them to death at a private family affair, like we do with people who sleep with their in-laws (Lev. 20:14)?

I know you have studied these things extensively, so I am confident you can help. Thank you again for reminding us that God's word is eternal and unchanging.

Your devoted disciple and adoring fan.

THE WORLD'S GREATEST EMAIL JOKE BOOK

---————— Original Message ————---

From: webbo
To: willis
Sent: Tuesday, February 18, 2003 11:47 AM
Subject: FW: Holy soap dispenser

Two priests are off to the showers late one night. They undress and step into the shower before they realise there is no soap. Father John says he has soap in his room and goes to get it, not bothering to dress. He grabs two bars of soap, one in each hand, and heads back to the showers. He is halfway down the hall when he sees three nuns heading his way. Having no place to hide, he stands against the wall and freezes like he's a statue.

The nuns stop and comment on how life like he looks. The first nun suddenly reaches out and pulls on his manhood. Startled, he drops a bar of soap. 'Oh look,' says the first nun, 'it's a soap dispenser.' To test her theory the second nun also pulls on his manhood. And sure enough, he drops the second bar of soap. The third nun decides to have a go. She pulls once, then twice and three times but nothing happens. So she gives it several more tugs, then yells out, 'Mary, Mother of God – hand lotion too!'

RELIGION

---------- Original Message ----------

From: webbo
To: willis
Sent: Friday, September 13, 2002 4:48 PM
Subject: FW: Treating the servants well

A Jewish girl tells her Catholic college roommate that she's going home for Rosh Hashanah.

The Catholic girl asks the Jewish girl, 'Is that the holiday when you light the candles?'

'No,' the Jewish girl replies. 'That's Chanukah.'

The Catholic girl then asks the Jewish girl, 'Is that the holiday when you eat the unleavened bread?'

'No,' the Jewish girl replies. 'That's Passover. Rosh Hashanah is the holiday when we blow the shofar.'

'See,' the Catholic Girl replies. 'That's what I like about you Jews ... you're so good to your servants.'

THE WORLD'S GREATEST EMAIL JOKE BOOK

———————— Original Message ————————

From: willis
To: webbo
Sent: Friday, February 07, 2003 12:00 AM
Subject: A question of faith

An Irish girl went to London to work as a secretary and began sending home money and gifts to her parents. After a few years they asked her to come home for a visit, as her elderly father was getting frail and very hard of hearing. She pulled up to the family home in a Rolls Royce and stepped out wearing diamonds and a full-length fur coat. As she walked into the house her father said, 'Hmm – they seem to be paying secretaries awfully well in London these days.'

The girl took his hands and said, 'Dad, I've been meaning to tell you something for years but I didn't want to put it in a letter. Obviously I can't hide it from you any longer. I've become a prostitute.' Her father gasped, put his hand on his chest and keeled over. The doctor was called but the old man had clearly lost the will to live. He was put to bed and the priest was called.

As the priest administered the Last Rites, with the mother and daughter weeping and wailing nearby, the old man muttered weakly, 'I'm a goner – killed by my own daughter! Killed by the shame of what she's become!'

RELIGION

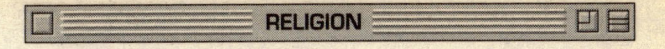

'Please forgive me,' his daughter sobbed, 'I only wanted to have nice things! I wanted to send you money and the only way I could do it was by becoming a prostitute.'

'PROSTITUTE?' The old man sat bolt upright in bed, smiling. 'Did you say PROSTITUTE? I thought you said PROTESTANT.'

THE WORLD'S GREATEST EMAIL JOKE BOOK

---------- Original Message ----------

From: webbo
To: willis
Sent: Friday, August 25, 2000 2:23 PM
Subject: The brothel

Two Irishmen were sitting in a pub having a beer and watching the brothel across the street. They saw a Baptist minister walk into the brothel, and one of them said, 'Aye, 'tis a shame to see a man of the cloth goin' bad.' Then they saw a rabbi enter the brothel, and the other Irishman said, 'Aye, 'tis a shame to see that the Jews are fallin' victim to temptation.' Then they saw a Catholic priest enter the brothel, and one of the Irishmen said, 'What a terrible pity… one of the girls must be quite ill.'

RELIGION

---——— Original Message ———---

From: webbo
To: willis
Sent: Wednesday, June 26, 2002 10:12 PM
Subject: The lost chapter of Genesis

Adam was hanging around the Garden of Eden, feeling very lonely. So God asked him, 'What's wrong with you?' Adam said he didn't have anyone to talk to.

God said that He was going to make Adam a companion and that it would be a woman. He said, 'This pretty lady will gather food for you, she will cook for you and, when you discover clothing, she will wash it for you. She will always agree with every decision you make, she will not nag you and will always be the first to admit she was wrong when you've had a disagreement. She will praise you! She will bear your children and never ask you to get up in the middle of the night to take care of them. She will never have a headache and will freely give you love and passion whenever you need it.'

Adam asked God, 'What will a woman like this cost?'
God replied, 'An arm and a leg.'
Then Adam asked, 'What can I get for a rib?'
Of course, the rest is history...

THE WORLD'S GREATEST EMAIL JOKE BOOK

———————— Original Message ————————

From: willis
To: webbo
Sent: Wednesday, May 01, 2002 11:38 AM
Subject: The St Peter challenge

Freddie Mercury, Gianni Versace and the Queen Mum arrive at the Pearly Gates. St Peter explains that only one can get through and that they each have to put forward their case for entry.

Freddie says, 'I know I haven't led a perfect life and I've made some mistakes along the way, but I've made some of the most beautiful music in the world. I'll stand at the back of heaven and serenade everybody with my wondrous songs, making heaven a far happier place to be.'

'Pretty good, Fred,' said St Peter. 'What about you, Gianni?'

Versace says, 'I make the most beautiful clothes in the world. I will completely redesign the fashions up here, from the archangels to the cherubs to the choirboys. As you well know, Pete, if you look good, you will feel good, and that will make heaven a much happier place.'

'Not bad,' says St Peter. 'What about you, Queen Mum?'

RELIGION

The Queen Mum does not say a word, instead she lifts up her skirt and pulls down her knickers, inserts a full bottle of Evian water into her vag, lets the water shoot up inside her and then gush out all over the floor.

'Excellent, you're in,' says St Peter.

'Hold on a f***ing minute,' says Freddie. 'She didn't even say anything.'

'Fred, you know the rules,' says St Peter. 'A royal flush beats a pair of queens…'

———————— Original Message ————————

From: webbo
To: willis
Sent: Wednesday, November 08, 2000 1:25 PM
Subject: FW: New York cab driver

A preacher and a cab driver die at the same time. At the gates of Heaven, Saint Peter hands the preacher a small set of white wings, then hands the cabby a large set of gold wings.

'Why does that cabby get gold wings?' asks the preacher. Saint Peter replies, 'While you were preaching, people were sleeping. While he was driving, people were praying!'

THE WORLD'S GREATEST EMAIL JOKE BOOK

———————— Original Message ————————

From: webbo
To: willis
Sent: Monday, May 21, 2001 12:07 PM
Subject: FW: Divine messages

God vs Government

A little boy wanted $100 badly and prayed for two weeks but nothing happened. Then he decided to write God a letter requesting the $100. When the postal authorities received the letter addressed to God USA, they decided to send it to President Bush. The President was so impressed, touched and amused that he instructed his secretary to send the little boy a $5 bill. The President thought this would appear to be a lot of money to a little boy. The little boy was delighted with the $5 and sat down to write a thank-you note to God, which read:

Dear God,
Thank you very much for sending the money. However, I noticed that for some reason you had to send it through Washington DC and, as usual, they took most of it.

RELIGION

The Queen and the Pope

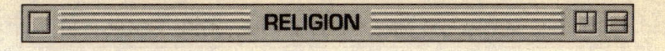

The Queen and the Pope are standing on the balcony of Buckingham Palace in front of gathered thousands. Out of the side of her mouth the Queen says to the Pope, 'I'll bet you two Swiss guards that with one small wave of my hand I can make every English person in the crowd go mad with delight.'

'OK,' whispers the Pope, 'this I want to see.'

So the Queen waves, and the crowd goes wild, nearly ripping their flags with joy. The Pope is impressed, but is not to be outdone.

'All right,' he says to the Queen out of the corner of his mouth, 'I'll bet you two Beefeaters that with one small nod of my head I can make every Australian person in the crowd go insane with adulation and celebrate for days.'

The Queen is certain that she's on to a winner here, so she whispers, 'Go on then.'

So the Pope headbutts her.

THE WORLD'S GREATEST EMAIL JOKE BOOK

---------- Original Message ----------

From: webbo
To: willis
Sent: Friday, August 25, 2000 2:23 PM
Subject: FW: Have you seen...

A drunk stumbles along a baptismal service down by the river on a Sunday afternoon. He proceeds to stumble down into the water and stands next to the minister. The minister turns, notices the old drunk and says, 'Mister, are you ready to find Jesus?'
The drunk looks back and says, 'Yes, sir, I am.'
The minister then dunks the fellow under the water and pulls him right back up. 'Have you found Jesus?' he asks.
'No, I haven't!' says the drunk.

The minister then dunks him under for a quite a while longer, brings him up and says, 'Now, brother, have you found Jesus?'
'No, I have not!' says the drunk again.
Disgusted, the minister holds the man under for at least 30 seconds, then brings him up and demands, 'For the grace of God, have you found Jesus yet?!'
The old drunk wipes his eyes and pleads, 'Are you sure this is where he fell in?'

RELIGION

―――――― Original Message ――――――

From: webbo
To: willis
Sent: Wednesday, October 11, 2000 1:30 PM
Subject: Lost in the desert

A nun and a priest were crossing the Sahara desert on a camel. On the third day, the camel suddenly dropped dead without warning. After dusting themselves off, the nun and the priest surveyed their situation. After a long period of silence, the priest spoke. 'Well, sister, this looks pretty grim.'
'I know, father.'
'In fact, I don't think it likely that we can survive more than a day or two.'
'I agree.'
'Sister, since we are unlikely to make it out of here alive, would you do something for me?'
'Anything, father.'
'I have never seen a woman's breasts and I was wondering if I might see yours.'
'Well, under the circumstances I don't see that it would do any harm.'
The nun opened her habit and the priest enjoyed the sight of her shapely breasts, commenting frequently on their beauty.
'Sister, would you mind if I touched them?'
She consented and he fondled them for several minutes.
'Father, could I ask something of you?'

'Yes, sister?'

'I have never seen a man's penis. Could I see yours?'

'I suppose that would be OK,' the priest replied, lifting his robe.

'Oh, father, may I touch it?'

The priest consented and after a few minutes of fondling he was sporting a huge erection. 'Sister, you know that, if I insert my penis in the right place, it can give life.'

'Is that true, father?'

'Yes, it is, sister.'

'Then why don't you stick it up that camel's ass and let's get the hell out of here.'

RELIGION

―――――― Original Message ――――――

From: webbo
To: willis
Sent: Monday, February 12, 2001 11:37 AM
Subject: FW: Taking a breather

There was a very strict church, which took periodic abstinence from sex as a qualification for church membership.
The pastor went up to the middle-aged couple and asked, 'Well, were you able to abstain from sex for the two weeks?'
The man replied, 'The first week wasn't too bad. The second week I had to sleep on the couch for a couple of nights, but yes, we made it.'
'Congratulations! Welcome to the church!' said the pastor.
The pastor then went up to the newly wed couple and asked, 'Well, were you able to abstain from sex for two weeks?'
'No, Pastor, we were not able to go without sex for the two weeks,' the young man replied sadly.
'What happened?' enquired the pastor.
'My wife was reaching for a can of paint on the top shelf and dropped it,' the man explained. 'When she bent over to pick it up, I was overcome with lust and took advantage of her right there.'
'You understand, of course, this means you will not be welcome in our church,' stated the pastor.

THE WORLD'S GREATEST EMAIL JOKE BOOK

'We know,' said the young man. 'We're not welcome at Homebase any more, either.'

➤ Technical Support

——————— Original Message ———————

From: willis
To: webbo
Sent: Monday, May 19, 2003 1:58 PM
Subject: FW: Virus warning

There is a new virus. The code name is 'work'. If you receive 'work' from your boss, your colleagues, via e-mail or anyone else, do not touch 'work' under any circumstances. This virus wipes out your private life completely.

If you should happen to come in contact with this virus, put on your jacket, take two good friends and go straight to the nearest pub. Order three drinks and after repeating 14 times, you will find that 'work' has been completely deleted from your brain.

Forward this virus warning immediately to at least five

friends. Should you realise that you do not have five friends, this means you are already infected with this virus and 'work' already controls your whole life.

——————————— Original Message ———————————

From: willis
To: webbo
Sent: Monday, April 29, 2002 12:40 PM
Subject: FW: Binary numbers

There are only 10 different types of people in the world: those who understand binary numbers and those who don't.

——————————— Original Message ———————————

From: willis
To: webbo
Sent: Wednesday, June 27, 2001 3:25 PM
Subject: FW: Quote of the century

'Computer games don't affect kids; I mean if Pac-Man affected us as kids, we'd all be running around in darkened rooms, munching magic pills and listening to repetitive electronic music.'
Kristian Wilson, Nintendo Inc, 1989

```
┌─────────────────────────────────────────────┐
│ ▭  ≡≡≡     TECHNICAL SUPPORT    ≡≡≡   ⌹ ⊟  │
└─────────────────────────────────────────────┘
```

──────────────── Original Message ────────────────

From: webbo
To: willis
Sent: Sunday, January 21, 2001 7:12 PM
Subject: FW: Haiku alerts

In Japan they have replaced the impersonal and unhelpful Microsoft 'error messages' with their own Japanese haiku poetry, each only 17 syllables: five syllables in the first line, seven in the second and five in the third.

Your file was so big.
It might be very useful.
But now it is gone.

The Web site you seek
Cannot be located,
But countless more exist.

Chaos reigns within.
Reflect, repent, and reboot.
Order shall return.

ABORTED effort:
Close all that you have worked on.
You ask far too much.

THE WORLD'S GREATEST EMAIL JOKE BOOK

Windows NT crashed.
I am the Blue Screen of Death.
No one hears your screams.

Yesterday it worked.
Today it is not working.
Windows is like that.

First snow, then silence.
This thousand-dollar screen dies
So beautifully.

With searching comes loss
And the presence of absence:
'My Novel' not found.

The Tao that is seen
Is not the true Tao – until
You bring fresh toner.

Stay the patient course.
Of little worth is your ire.
The network is down.

A crash reduces
Your expensive computer
To a simple stone.

TECHNICAL SUPPORT

Three things are certain:
Death, taxes and lost data.
Guess which has occurred.

You step in the stream,
But the water has moved on.
This page is not here.

Out of memory.
We wish to hold the whole sky,
But we never will.

Having been erased,
The document you're seeking
Must now be retyped.

Serious error.
All shortcuts have disappeared.
Screen. Mind. Both are blank.

THE WORLD'S GREATEST EMAIL JOKE BOOK

———————— Original Message ————————

From: willis
To: webbo
Sent: Saturday, January 27, 2001 10:20 AM
Subject: Non-starter

Here is an apparently real conversation that was transcribed from a recording monitoring the customer-care department of a helpline:

'Computer assistance. May I help you?'
'Yes, well, I'm having trouble with WordPerfect.'
'What sort of trouble?'
'Well, I was just typing along, and all of a sudden the words went away.'
'Went away?'
'They disappeared.'
'Hmm. So what does your screen look like now?'
'Nothing.'
'Nothing?'
'It's blank. It won't accept anything when I type.'
'Are you still in WordPerfect, or did you get out?'
'How do I tell?'
'Can you see the C: prompt on the screen?'
'What's a sea prompt?'
'Never mind. Can you move your cursor around the screen?'
'There isn't any cursor. I told you, it won't accept anything I type.'

TECHNICAL SUPPORT

'Does your monitor have a power indicator?'
'What's a monitor?'
'It's the thing with the screen on it that looks like a TV. Does it have a little light that tells you when it's on?'
'I don't know.'
'Well, then look on the back of the monitor and find where the power cord goes into it. Can you see that?'
'Yes, I think so.'
'Great. Follow the cord to the plug, and tell me if it's plugged into the wall.'
'Yes, it is.'
'When you were behind the monitor, did you notice that there were two cables plugged into the back of it, not just one?'
'No.'
'Well, there are. I need you to look back there again and find the other cable.'
'OK, here it is.'
'Follow it for me, and tell me if it's plugged securely into the back of your computer.'
'I can't reach.'
'Uh huh. Well, can you see if it is?'
'No.'
'Even if you maybe put your knee on something and lean way over?'
'Oh, it's not because I don't have the right angle – it's because it's dark.'
'Dark?'

'Yes. The office light is off, and the only light I have is coming in from the window.'
'Well, turn on the office light then.'
'I can't.'
'No? Why not?'
'Because there's a power failure.'
'A power... A power failure? Aha. OK, we've got it under control. Do you still have the boxes and manuals and packing stuff your computer came in?'
'Well, yes, I keep them in the cupboard.'
'Good. Go get them, unplug your system and pack it up just like it was when you got it. Then take it back to the store you bought it from.'
'Really? Is it that bad?'
'Yes, I'm afraid it is.'
'Well, all right then, I suppose. What do I tell them?'
'Tell them you're too stupid to own a computer.'

TECHNICAL SUPPORT

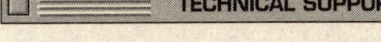

──────────── Original Message ────────────

```
From: willis
To: webbo
Sent: Friday, June 13, 2003 4:37 PM
Subject: FW: Baffled by technology
```

Take heart, anyone among you who believes they are technologically challenged – you ain't seen nothing yet! This is an excerpt from a *Wall Street Journal* article:

1. Compaq is considering changing the command 'Press Any Key' to 'Press Return Key' because of the flood of calls asking where the 'Any' key is.

2. AST technical support had a caller complaining that her mouse was hard to control with the dust cover on. The cover turned out to be the plastic bag the mouse was packaged in.

3. Another Dell customer called to say he couldn't get his computer to fax anything. After 40 minutes of troubleshooting, the technician discovered the man was trying to fax a piece of paper by holding it in front of the monitor screen and hitting the 'Send' key.

4. Yet another Dell customer called to complain that his keyboard no longer worked. He had cleaned it by filling up his bathtub with soap and water and

soaking the keyboard for a day, then removing all the keys and washing them individually.

5. A Dell technician received a call from a customer who was enraged because his computer had told him he was 'bad and an invalid'. The technician explained that the computer's 'bad command' and 'invalid' responses shouldn't be taken personally.

6. A confused caller to IBM was having trouble printing documents. He told the technician that the computer had said it 'couldn't find printer'. The user said he had tried turning the computer screen to face the printer but his computer still couldn't 'see' the printer.

7. An exasperated caller to Dell computer tech support couldn't get her new Dell computer to turn on. After ensuring the computer was plugged in, the technician asked her what happened when she pushed the power button. Her response was, 'I pushed and pushed on this foot pedal and nothing happened.' The 'foot pedal' turned out to be the computer's mouse…

8. Another customer called Compaq tech support to say her brand new computer wouldn't work. She said she unpacked the unit, plugged it in and sat there for 20 minutes waiting for something

TECHNICAL SUPPORT

to happen. When asked what happened when she pressed the power switch, she asked, 'What power switch?'

9. Another IBM customer had trouble installing software and rang for support. 'I put in the first disc, and that was OK. It said to put in the second disc, and had some problems with it. When it said to put in the third disc, I couldn't even fit it in...' The user hadn't realised that 'insert disc 2' implied removing disc 1 first.

10. A story from a Novell NetWire SysOp:
Caller: 'Hello, is this tech support?'
Tech support: 'Yes, it is. How may I help you?'
Caller: 'The cup holder on my PC is broken – and I am within my warranty period. How do I go about getting that fixed?'
Tech support: 'I'm sorry, but did you say a cup holder?'
Caller: 'Yes, it's attached to the front of my computer.'
Tech support: 'Please excuse me. If I seem a bit stumped, it's because I am. Did you receive this as part of a promotional at a trade show? How did you get this cup holder? Does it have any trademark on it?'
Caller: 'It came with my computer. I don't know anything about a promotional. It just has "4X" on it.'
At this point, the technician had to mute the caller

because he couldn't stand it. He was laughing too hard. The caller had been using the load drawer of the CD-ROM drive as a cup holder and it had snapped it off the drive.

11. A woman called the Canon helpdesk with a problem with her printer.
    The technician asked her if she was 'running it under Windows'. The woman responded, 'No, my desk is next to the door. But that is a good point. The man sitting in the cubicle next to me is under a window and his printer is working fine.'

12. And last but not least:
    Tech support: 'OK, Bob, let's press the Control and Escape keys at the same time. That brings up a task list in the middle of the screen. Now type the letter "P" to bring up the Program Manager.'
    Customer: 'I don't have a "P".'
    Tech support: 'On your keyboard, Bob.'
    Customer: 'What do you mean?'
    Tech support: '"P" on your keyboard, Bob.'
    Customer: 'I'm not going to do that!'

TECHNICAL SUPPORT

———————— Original Message ————————

From: webbo
To: willis
Sent: Tuesday, June 03, 2003 9:59 AM
Subject: FW: Rolls Royce experiment

Sometimes it really does take a rocket scientist!

Scientists at an aeroplane engine factory built a gun specifically to launch dead chickens at the windshields of airliners and military jets, all travelling at maximum velocity. The idea was to simulate the frequent incidents of collisions with airborne fowl to test the strength of the windshields.

American engineers heard about the gun and were eager to test it on the windshields of their new high-speed trains. Arrangements were made and a gun was sent to the American engineers. When the gun was fired, the engineers stood shocked as the chicken hurled out of the barrel, crashed into the shatterproof shield, smashed it to smithereens, blasted through the control console, snapped the engineer's back-rest in two, and embedded itself in the back wall of the cabin like an arrow shot from a bow.

The horrified Americans sent the factory the disastrous results of the experiment, along with the designs of the windshield and begged the British scientists for suggestions. Rolls Royce responded with a one-line memo: 'Defrost the chicken.'

──────── Original Message ────────

From: willis
To: webbo
Sent: Monday, May 13, 2002 11:21 AM
Subject: FW: Bill Gates at the Pearly Gates

For all who get frustrated with the computer...

'Well, Bill,' said God, 'I'm really confused about this one. I'm not sure whether to send you to Heaven or Hell! After all, you helped society enormously by putting a computer in almost every home in the world, and yet you created that ghastly Windows. I'm going to do something I've never done before. I'm going to let you decide where you want to go!'
'Well, thanks, God,' Bill replied. 'What's the difference between the two?'
'You can take a brief peek at both places, if it will help you decide,' said God. 'Shall we look at Hell first?'
'Sure!' said Bill. 'Let's go!'
Bill was amazed! He saw a clean, white sandy beach with clear waters. There were thousands of beautiful women running around, playing in the water, laughing

TECHNICAL SUPPORT

and frolicking about. The sun was shining and the temperature was perfect!

'This is great!' sad Bill. 'If this is Hell, I can't wait to see Heaven!'

To which God replied, 'Let's go!' And off they went.

Bill saw puffy white clouds in a beautiful blue sky, with angels drifting about playing harps and singing. It was nice, but surely not as enticing as Hell. Mr Gates thought for only a brief moment and announced his decision.

'God, I do believe I would like to go to Hell.'

'As you desire,' said God.

Two weeks later, God decided to check up on the late billionaire to see how things were going. He found Bill shackled to a wall, screaming among the hot flames in a dark cave. He was being burned and tortured by demons.

'How ya doin', Bill?' asked God.

Bill responded with anguish and despair. 'This is awful! This is not what I expected at all! What happened to the beach and the beautiful women playing in the water?'

'Oh THAT!' said God. 'That was the screen saver!'

Brotherly Love

---————— Original Message ———---

From: willis
To: webbo
Sent: Tuesday, November 28, 2000 11:18 AM
Subject: FW: Three wishes

Three guys – an Englishman, a Frenchman and an American – were out walking along the beach together one day. They came across a lantern and a genie popped out of it.
'I will give you each one wish,' said the genie.
The American said, 'I am a farmer, my dad was a farmer, and my son will also farm. I want the land to be forever fertile in America.'
And with a blink of the genie's eye, FOOM! The land in America was made forever fertile for farming.
The Frenchman was amazed, so he said, 'I want a wall around France so that no one can come into our precious country.'

THE WORLD'S GREATEST EMAIL JOKE BOOK

Again, with a blink of the genie's eye, POOF! There was a huge wall around France.

'I'm very curious,' the Englishman said. 'Please tell me more about this wall.'

So the genie explained, 'Well, it's about 45 metres high, 15 metres thick and nothing can get in or out.'

'Fill it up with water,' replied the Englishman.

——————————— Original Message ———————————

From: willis
To: webbo
Sent: Friday, September 06, 2002 3:39 PM
Subject: FW: Survey

Last month, in preparation for the Earth Summit currently being hosted by South Africa, the UN conducted a worldwide survey. The only question was: 'Would you please give your honest opinion about solutions to the food shortage in the rest of the world?' The survey was a huge failure… In Africa, they didn't know what 'food' meant. In Eastern Europe, they didn't know what 'honest' meant. In Western Europe, they didn't know what 'shortage' meant. In China, they didn't know what 'opinion' meant. In the Middle East, they didn't know what 'solutions' meant. In South America, they didn't know what 'please' meant. And in the US, they didn't know what 'the rest of the world' meant.

BROTHERLY LOVE

---------- Original Message ----------

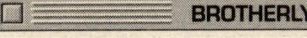

From: willis
To: webbo
Sent: Tuesday, June 19, 2001 6:56 PM
Subject: Bob Hope

Bob Hope appeared on British TV show *Surprise, Surprise* and bragged that, despite his 97 years of age, he could still have sex three times a night. After the show, a Liverpudlian production girl said, 'Bob, if I'm not being too forward, I'd love to have sex with an older man. Let's go back to my place.' So they went back to her place and had great sex.

Afterwards, Bob said, 'If you think that was good, let me sleep for half an hour, and we can have even better sex. But while I'm sleeping, hold my testicles in your left hand and my penis in your right hand.' the girl looked a bit perplexed, but said, 'OK.'

After half an hour Bob woke up, and they had even better sex. Then Bob said, 'That was wonderful. But, if you let me sleep for an hour, we can have the best sex yet. But again, hold my testicles in your left hand and my penis in your right hand.'

'Great, Bob,' said the girl, 'but tell me, does my holding your testicles in my left hand and your penis in my right stimulate you while you're sleeping?'

Bob replied, 'No, but the last time I slept with a Scouser, she stole my wallet!'

―――――― Original Message ――――――

From: willis
To: webbo
Sent: Wednesday, May 01, 2002 10:19 PM
Subject: Geography lesson

The geography of a woman:

Between the ages of 18 and 21, a woman is like Africa or Australia. She is half discovered, half wild and naturally beautiful, with bush land around the fertile deltas.

Between the ages of 21 and 30, a woman is like America or Japan. Completely discovered, very well developed and open to trade, especially with countries with cash or cars.

Between the ages of 30 and 35, she is like India or Spain. Very hot, relaxed and convinced of her own beauty.

Between the ages of 35 and 40, a woman is like France or Argentina. She may have been half destroyed during the war but can still be a warm and desirable place to visit.

Between the ages of 40 and 50, she is like Yugoslavia or Iraq. She lost the war and is haunted by past mistakes. Massive reconstruction is now necessary.

BROTHERLY LOVE

Between the ages of 50 and 60, she is like Russia or Canada. Very wide, quiet and the borders are practically unpatrolled but the frigid climate keeps people away.

Between the ages of 60 and 70, a woman is like England or Mongolia. With a glorious and all-conquering past but alas no future.

After 70, women become like Albania or Afghanistan. Everyone knows where she is, but no one wants to go there.

The geography of a man:

Between the ages of 15 and 70, a man is like Zimbabwe. Ruled by a dick.

```
-------- Original Message --------
From: webbo
To: willis
Sent: Monday, March 24, 2003 11:52 AM
Subject: FW: St Paddy's is coming!
```

Irish predicament:

Ole Mulvihill (from the Northern Irish clan) staggers drunk into a Catholic church, enters a confessional box and sits down but says nothing. The priest coughs a few times to get his attention, but Ole just sits there. Finally, the priest pounds three times on the wall. The drunk mumbles, 'Ain't no use knockin'. There's no paper on this side either.'

Irish last request:

Mary Clancy goes up to Father O'Grady's after his Sunday morning service, and she's in tears.
'So what's bothering you, Mary, my dear?' asks the priest.
'Oh, Father, I've got terrible news,' says Mary. 'My husband passed away last night.'
'Oh, Mary, that's terrible. Tell me, did he have any last requests?'
'That he did, Father...' she says.
'What did he ask, Mary?'
'He said, "Please, Mary, put down that damn gun!"'

BROTHERLY LOVE

---------- Original Message ----------

From: willis
To: webbo
Sent: Friday, January 31, 2003 2:09 PM
Subject: Eminem

Eminem's tour of Ireland is to go ahead, despite concerns over a sickening attitude to women, appallingly obscene language, an irresponsible attitude to sex and violence, and of course the booze. But Eminem said that, despite these shocking traits, he would wait and judge the Irish for himself.

---------- Original Message ----------

From: webbo
To: willis
Sent: Wednesday, October 18, 2000 10:07 AM
Subject: FW: Air crash

Ireland's worst air disaster occurred today when a small two-seater plane crashed into a cemetery in central Ireland this afternoon. Irish search and rescue workers have recovered 826 bodies so far and expect that number to climb as digging continues into the night.

THE WORLD'S GREATEST EMAIL JOKE BOOK

———————— Original Message ————————

From: webbo
To: willis
Sent: Thursday, November 16, 2000 9:59 AM
Subject: Dear America...

Notice of Revocation of Independence

To the citizens of the United States of America,

In the light of your failure to elect a president of the USA and thus to govern yourselves, we hereby give notice of the revocation of your independence, effective as of today. Her Sovereign Majesty Queen Elizabeth II will resume monarchial duties over all states, commonwealths and other territories. Except Utah, which she does not fancy. Your new prime minister (the Right Honourable Tony Blair, MP, for the 97.85% of you who until now have been unaware that there is a world outside your borders) will appoint a minister for America without the need for further elections. Congress and the Senate will be disbanded. A questionnaire will be circulated next year to determine whether any of you noticed.

To aid in the transition to a British Crown Dependency, the following rules are introduced with immediate effect:

1. You should look up 'revocation' in the *Oxford English*

BROTHERLY LOVE

Dictionary. Then look up 'aluminium'. Check the pronunciation guide. You will be amazed at just how wrongly you have been pronouncing it. Generally, you should raise your vocabulary to acceptable levels. Look up 'vocabulary'. Using the same 27 words interspersed with filler noises such as 'like' and 'you know' is an unacceptable and inefficient form of communication. Look up 'interspersed'.

2. There is no such thing as 'American' English. We will let Microsoft know on your behalf.

3. You should learn to distinguish the English and Australian accents. It really isn't that hard.

4. Occasionally Hollywood will be required to cast English actors as the good guys.

5. You should relearn your original national anthem, 'God Save The Queen', but only after fully carrying out task one. We would not want you to get confused and give up halfway through.

6. You should stop playing American football. There is only one kind of football. What you refer to as American football is not a very good game. The 2.15% of you who are aware that there is a world outside your borders may have noticed that no one else plays American football. You will no longer be allowed to play it, and should instead play proper football. Initially, it would be best if you played with the girls. It is a difficult game. Those of you brave enough will, in time, be allowed to play rugby (which is similar to American football, but does not involve stopping for a rest every 20 seconds or wearing full Kevlar body armour like nancies). We are hoping to get together at least a US rugby sevens side by 2005.

7. You should declare war on Quebec and France, using nuclear weapons if they give you any merde. The 98.85% of you who were not aware that there is a world outside your borders should count yourselves lucky. The Russians have never been the bad guys. 'Merde' is French for 'shit'.

8. July 4 is no longer a public holiday. November 8 will be a new national holiday, but only in England. It will be called 'Indecisive Day'.

9. All American cars are hereby banned. It is for your own good — they are crap. When we show you German cars, you will understand what we mean.

10. Please tell us who killed JFK. It's been driving us crazy.

Thank you for your co-operation.

BROTHERLY LOVE

———————— Original Message ————————

From: willis
To: webbo
Sent: Thursday, November 16, 2000 1:34 PM
Subject: FW: Serbia sends peacekeeping troops to the US

Belgrade:

Serbian president Vojislav Kostunica deployed more than 30,000 peacekeeping troops to the US on Monday, pledging full support to the troubled North American nation as it struggles to establish democracy. 'We must do all we can to support free elections in America and allow democracy to gain a foothold there,' Kostunica said. 'The US is a major player in the western hemisphere and its continued stability is vital to Serbian interests in that region.'

Kostunica urged Al Gore, the US opposition-party leader who is refusing to recognise the nation's 7 November election results, to 'let the democratic process take its course'. 'Mr Gore needs to acknowledge the will of the people and concede that he has lost this election,' Kostunica said. 'Until America's political figures learn to respect the institutions that have been put in place, the nation will never be a true democracy.'

THE WORLD'S GREATEST EMAIL JOKE BOOK

Serbian forces have been stationed throughout the US, with an emphasis on certain trouble zones. Among them are Oregon, Florida and eastern Tennessee, where Gore set up headquarters in Bush territory. An additional 10,000 troops are expected to arrive in the capital city of Washington DC by Friday.

Although Kostunica has pledged to work with US leaders, he did not rule out the possibility of economic sanctions if the crisis is not resolved soon. 'For democracy to take root and flourish, it must be planted in the rich soil of liberty. And the cornerstone of liberty is elections free of tampering or corruption,' said Kostunica. 'Should America prove itself incapable of learning this lesson on its own, the international community may be forced to take stronger measures.'

| BROTHERLY LOVE |

———————— Original Message ————————

From: webbo
To: willis
Sent: Thursday, November 16, 2000 2:11 PM
Subject: FW: Dear Britain...

Re: Notice of Revocation of Independence

To the subjects of the British 'Queen',

We, the people of the Untied States of America, do hereby resolve to once again state our independence from any country that puts meat in a pie. However, due to the fact that you gave the world the Beatles and kept Adam Ant to yourselves, we will give you Utah. Maybe you guys can find a use for the Osmonds.

As correctly stated in your broadside, 2.15% of us do realise there is a world out there. Therefore, our desire to join the ranks of illiterate sheep farmers in the Falklands, destitute residents of Tristan de Cuhna, chronically depressed islanders of St Helena and the forgotten folk on Pitcairn cannot be characterised as burning. To be in the same league as one of those poor slobs living at the foot of Gibraltar is something that we can do without. However, we might be able to make a deal concerning sending the above-mentioned Osmonds on a world tour of the 'empire'. As a sign of goodwill and in the hope that we can also do something good for the mother country, we would be willing to allow Gary Glitter to open the show.

As we will not be needing someone to administrate the monarchal despotism, Mr Blair need not expend his energy searching for a minister. However, if you guys really need a minister, Jimmy Swaggart might be available.

As to the rules governing a crown dependency:

1) Don't hold any sermons about pronunciation. Less than 2.15% of your countrymen are unable to get any recognisable word out of their mouths. And if you'd get your nose out of the air for a minute and just consider your vocabulary, we might get somewhere. A 'bonnet' is something you put on your head. A 'mate' is somebody you make babies with. A 'Z' is a zee – the Eurotrash pronunciation we can do without.

2) A contradiction. Either there is 'American' English or no Microsoft – you can't have it both ways.

3) Distinguishing between English and Australian accents – get serious! Not even the Australians care!

4) I'm sure you'll agree that Scottish, Welsh and Northern Irish actors will have the advantage of the equal opportunity laws. Besides, Hugh Grant is

BROTHERLY LOVE

always good for a laugh and we gave citizenship to Cary Grant and Bob Hope.

5) How about if we make one anthem for two countries: 'This Land is Your Land', from Woody Guthrie, for the UK and the States, and 'Candle in the Wind' for Canada?

6) Here's the deal. We stop playing American football and you give refugee status to all the soccer moms that we send back to the mother country.

7) No problem here. War has been declared. However, the UK will have to listen to all (former) French pop acts.

8) Also no problem. We will, however, continue to go to the beach and drink beer on 4 July. We'd prefer if all of you would stay away from our shores during this time. English people in bathing suits are simply disgusting. Blue skin that tends to crisp instead of tan – yuck.

9) Oh great, we can all drive a Rover or a Mini. Another typical example of the British way to win friends.

10) It was Andrew Lloyd Webber. Now tell us, who's going to kill him?

THE WORLD'S GREATEST EMAIL JOKE BOOK

──────── Original Message ────────

From: webbo
To: willis
Sent: Friday, November 24, 2000 12:34 PM
Subject: Newsflash

Japan has sent 50,000,000 cases of Viagra to the US. It heard that the entire country can't get an election.

──────── Original Message ────────

From: webbo
To: willis
Sent: Tuesday, April 01, 2003 8:29 PM
Subject: FW: Evidence

News reports have filtered out early this morning that US forces have swooped on an Iraqi primary school and detained secondary-school teacher Mohammed Al-Hazar. Sources indicate that, when arrested, Al-Hazar was in possession of a ruler, a protractor, a set square and a calculator. US President George W Bush argued that this was clear and overwhelming evidence that Iraq indeed possessed weapons of maths instruction.

BROTHERLY LOVE

— Original Message —

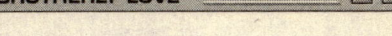

From: webbo
To: willis
Sent: Tuesday, March 25, 2003 5:29 PM
Subject: US - French relations

'I would rather have a German division in front of me than a French one behind me.'
US General George S Patton

'Going to war without France is like going deer hunting without your accordion.'
US General Norman Schwarzkopf

'We can stand here like the French, or we can do something about it.'
US President Dwight Eisenhower

'As far as I'm concerned, war always means failure.'
Jacques Chirac, President of France

'As far as France is concerned, you're right.'
US Senator Bob Dole

'The only time France wants us to go to war is when the German Army is sitting in Paris sipping coffee.'
US TV chat-show host Regis Philbin

'I don't know why people are surprised that France won't help us get Saddam out of Iraq. After all, France wouldn't help us get the Germans out of France!'
US TV talk-show host Jay Leno

'The last time the French asked for "more proof" it came marching into Paris under a German flag.'
US TV talk-show host David Letterman

'You know why the French don't want to bomb Saddam Hussein? Because he hates America, he loves mistresses and wears a beret. He is French, people.'
US TV talk-show host Conan O'Brien

'War without France would be like… uh… World War II.'
US comedian Carrot Top

'What do you expect from a culture and a nation that exerted more of its national will to fighting against Disney World and Big Macs than the Nazis?'
US comedian Dennis Miller

'It is important to remember that the French have always been there when they needed us.'
US President John F Kennedy

BROTHERLY LOVE

———————— Original Message ————————

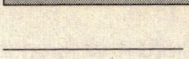

From: willis
To: webbo
Sent: Friday, September 27, 2002 2:57 PM
Subject: FW: Earthquake appeal

Urgent – Dudley Earthquake Appeal

At 00:54 on Monday 23 September an earthquake measuring 4.8 on the Richter scale hit Dudley in the West Midlands, causing untold disruption and distress:

* Many were woken well before their giro arrived.
* Several priceless collections of mementos from the Balearics and Spanish Costas were damaged.
* Three areas of historic and scientifically significant litter were disturbed.
* Thousands are confused and bewildered, trying to come to terms with the fact that something interesting has happened in Dudley.

How you can help:
* £2 buys chips, scraps and blue pop for a family of four.
* £10 can take a family to Stourport for the day, where children can play on an unspoiled canal bank among the national collection of stinging nettles.
* 22p buys a biro for filling in a spurious compensation claim.

THE WORLD'S GREATEST EMAIL JOKE BOOK

Please act now! Simply e-mail us by return with your credit card details and we'll do the rest!

---------- Original Message ----------

From: willis
To: webbo
Sent: Monday, June 03, 2002 11:48 AM
Subject: Globalisation

Question: What is the height of globalisation?
Answer: Princess Diana's death
Question: How come?
Answer: An English princess with an Egyptian boyfriend crashes in a French tunnel while travelling in a German car with a Dutch engine, driven by a Belgian who is pissed on Scotch whisky, followed closely by Italian paparazzi on Japanese motorcycles. Following the crash she is treated by an American doctor, using Brazilian medicines. And this is sent to you by a South African using Bill Gates's technology, which he stole from the Japanese.

BROTHERLY LOVE

--- Original Message ---

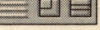

From: willis
To: webbo
Sent: Thursday, October 24, 2002 5:03 PM
Subject: FW: Report on Israel

A reporter for CNN goes to Israel to cover the fighting. She is looking for something of human interest, something emotional and positive; like the man in Sarajevo who every day risked his life to play cello in the town square. In Jerusalem she hears about an old Jew who has been going to the Western Wall to pray twice a day for a long, long time. So she goes to the Western Wall and there he is! She watches him pray and after about 45 minutes, when he turns to leave, she approaches him for an interview.

'Rebecca Smith, CNN News. Sir, how long have you been coming to the Western Wall to pray?'

'For about 50 years.'

'What do you pray for?'

'For peace between the Jews and the Arabs. For all the hatred to stop. For our children to grow up in safety and friendship.'

'How do you feel after doing this for 50 years?'

'Like I'm talking to a f**king wall…'

THE WORLD'S GREATEST EMAIL JOKE BOOK

──────── Original Message ────────

From: webbo
To: willis
Sent: Tuesday, May 14, 2002 8:44 PM
Subject: The best pub in the world

A Scotsman, an Italian and an Irishman are in a bar. They are having a good time, and all agree that the bar is a nice place. Then the Scotsman says, 'Aye, this is a nice bar, but where I come from, back in Glasgee, there's a better one. At MacDougal's, ye buy a drink, ye buy another drink, and MacDougal himself will buy yir third drink!' The others agree that sounds like a good place.

Then the Italian says, 'Yeah, dat's a nica bar, but where I come from, dere's a better one... In Roma, dere's this place, Vincenzo's. At Vincenzo's, you buy a drink, Vincenzo buys you a drink. You buy anudda drink, Vincenzo buys you anudda drink.' Everyone agrees that sounds like a great bar.

Finally the Irishman says, 'You tink dat's great? Where Oi come from in Oirland, dere's dis place called Morphy's. At Morphy's, dey boy you your forst drink, dey boy you your second drink, dey boy you your tird drink, and den dey take you in de back and get you laid!'
Wow!' say the other two, 'that's fantastic! Did that actually happen to you?'
'No,' replies the Irishman, 'but it happened to me sister!'

BROTHERLY LOVE

———————— Original Message ————————

From: willis
To: webbo
Sent: Monday, September 17, 2001 10:16 PM
Subject: Irish skipping

An Irishwoman is terribly overweight, so her doctor puts her on a diet. 'I want you to eat regularly for two days, then skip a day, and repeat this procedure for two weeks,' he instructs. 'The next time I see you, you'll have lost at least 2kg.'

When the Irishwoman returns, she shocks the doctor by losing nearly 9kg. 'Why, that's amazing!' the doctor says. 'Did you follow my instructions?'

The Irishwoman nods. 'I'll tell you though, I thought I was going to drop dead that third day.'

'From hunger, you mean?' asks the doctor. 'No, from skipping.'

THE WORLD'S GREATEST EMAIL JOKE BOOK

──────── Original Message ────────

From: webbo
To: willis
Sent: Tuesday, October 09, 2001 4:45 PM
Subject: FW: Scouser terrorists

The latest news reports advise that a cell of four terrorists has been operating in Merseyside, Liverpool. Earlier today, police announced that three of the four have been detained. The Merseyside Regional Police Commissioner stated that the terrorists Bin Sleepin', Bin Drinkin' and Bin Fightin' have been arrested on immigration issues. The police can find no one fitting the description of the fourth cell member, Bin Workin', in the area, but they are confident that anyone who looks like Workin' will be very easy to spot in the community.

BROTHERLY LOVE

---— Original Message ———

From: willis
To: webbo
Sent: Friday, November 22, 2002 9:40 PM
Subject: A word of advice

Yesterday, a friend of mine was travelling on a Paris to Birmingham flight. As they were leaving the plane my friend noticed that a man of Arabic appearance had left his bag behind. She grabbed the bag and ran after him. Finally she caught up with him in the terminal and handed back his bag. He was extremely grateful and reached into his bag, which appeared to contain large bundles of money. He looked around, to make sure nobody was looking, and whispered, 'I can never repay your kindness, but I will try to with a word of advice: Stay away from Liverpool.'

My friend was genuinely terrified. 'Is there going to be an attack?' she asked him.

'No,' he whispered back. 'It's a shithole.'

🗖 🗏 THE WORLD'S GREATEST EMAIL JOKE BOOK 🗏 🗗 🗏

———————— Original Message ————————

From: willis
To: webbo
Sent: Friday, July 21, 2000 4:09 PM
Subject: FW: No room at the barn...

One day a Jew, a Hindu and a Scouser all arrived at their hotel to find that there had been a mix-up with the bookings and there was only one room left for them to share. The manager explained that this room had only two beds but there was a barn at a neighbouring farm which the farmer, an old friend of his, would let one of them sleep in free of charge. They complained a little, but since there was nowhere else to go, the Jew graciously said he'd sleep in the barn.

The Hindu and the Scouser were just settling down to sleep in their room when there was a knock at the door. It was the Jew. 'I'm sorry,' he said, 'but there's a pig in that barn and because I'm Jewish I feel uncomfortable about sharing the barn with it.'

'No problem,' said the Hindu. 'I'll sleep out there instead.' So off he went to the barn, leaving the Scouser and the Jew to share the room.

They were just settling down to sleep when there was a knock at the door. It was the Hindu. 'I'm sorry,' he said, 'but there's a cow in that barn and because I'm a Hindu

BROTHERLY LOVE

I feel uncomfortable about sharing the barn with it.' The Scouser grudgingly agreed to give up his bed and stomped off to the barn, leaving the Jew and the Hindu to share the room.

The Jew and the Hindu were just settling down to sleep when there was a knock at the door. It was the cow and the pig.

---------- Original Message ----------

From: webbo
To: willis
Sent: Monday, January 15, 2001 11:18 AM
Subject: Designer croc

Two Scousers are fishing in South Africa, taking it easy, when a crocodile swims past with a bloke's head in its mouth. One Scouser says to the other, 'F**kin' 'ell, Terry, look at that bloke!' The other Scouser says, 'I know, Barry, the flash bastard's got a Lacoste sleeping bag.'

THE WORLD'S GREATEST EMAIL JOKE BOOK

———— Original Message ————

From: willis
To: webbo
Sent: Thursday, October 24, 2002 4:42 PM
Subject: Lost at sea

Two Irishmen, Patrick and Michael, were adrift in a lifeboat following a dramatic escape from a burning freighter. While rummaging through the boat's provisions, Patrick stumbled across an old lamp. Secretly hoping that a genie would appear, he rubbed the lamp vigorously. To his amazement, a genie came forth. This particular genie, however, stated that he could only deliver one wish, not the standard three. Without giving much thought to the matter, Patrick blurted out, 'Turn the entire ocean into Guinness!' The genie clapped his hands with a deafening crash, and immediately the entire sea turned into the finest brew ever sampled by mortals. Simultaneously the genie vanished. Only the gentle lapping of Guinness on the hull broke the stillness as the two men considered their circumstances. Michael looked disgustedly at Patrick, whose wish had been granted. After a long, tension-filled moment, he spoke. 'Nice going, Patrick! Now we're going to have to pee in the boat.'

BROTHERLY LOVE

―――――――― Original Message ――――――――

```
From: webbo
To: willis
Sent: Monday, January 22, 2001 11:35 AM
Subject: Colour-blind?
```

A black man talks to a white man:

'When I was born I was black,
When I grew up I was black,
When I'm sick I'm black,
When I go in the sun I'm black,
When I'm cold I'm black,
And when I die I'll be black.
But you: When you're born you're pink,
When you grow up you're white,
When you're sick you're green,
When you go in the sun you turn red,
When you're cold you turn blue,
And when you die you turn purple.
And you have the nerve to call me coloured.'

THE WORLD'S GREATEST EMAIL JOKE BOOK

---------- Original Message ----------

From: willis
To: webbo
Sent: Wednesday, May 19, 2004 10:32 PM
Subject: Irish sausage

Shamus and Murphy fancied a pint or two but, not having a lot of money between them, they could only raise the staggering sum of one euro. Murphy said, 'Hang on, I have an idea.' He went next door to the butcher's shop and came out with one large sausage.
'Are you crazy?' said Shamus. 'Now we don't have any money left at all!'
'Don't worry,' Murphy replied. 'Just follow me.'
They went into a pub, where Murphy immediately ordered two pints of Guinness and two glasses of Jameson whiskey.
'Now, you've lost it!' said Shamus. 'Do you know how much trouble we'll be in? We haven't got any money!'
'Don't worry, I have a plan,' Murphy replied with a smile. 'Cheers!'
The two men downed their drinks, then Murphy said, 'OK, I'll stick the sausage through my zipper. You get down on your knees and put it in your mouth.'
The barman noticed them, went berserk and threw them out.
Shamus and Murphy continued this ruse, pub after pub, getting more and more drunk, all free of charge. Finally, at the tenth pub Shamus said, 'Murphy, I don't think I can

do any more o' this. I'm drunk, and me knees are killin' me!'
'How do you think I feel?' said Murphy said. 'I lost the sausage in the third pub!'

General Smut

———————— Original Message ————————

From: webbo
To: willis
Sent: Wednesday, February 06, 2002 9:39 PM
Subject: The towel

An old man marries a young woman and they are deeply in love. However, no matter what the husband does sexually, the woman never achieves orgasm, so they decide to ask a sex therapist for advice.

The therapist listens to their story and makes a suggestion: 'Hire a strapping young man and, while the two of you are making love, have the young man wave a towel over you, as though he is fanning you both. Make sure he is totally naked and she can see his manhood as he fans you with the towel. That will help your wife fantasise, and should bring on a full-blown orgasm.'

The couple go home and follow the therapist's advice. They hire a handsome young man and he strips off and enthusiastically waves a towel over them both as they make love. But it doesn't help, and still the wife is unsatisfied and frustrated. Perplexed, they go back to the therapist. 'OK, let's try it reversed,' he says, turning to the husband. 'Have the young man make love to your wife and you wave the towel over them.'

Once again, they follow the advice. The young man gets into bed with the wife and the husband waves the towel. The hired hand really works with great enthusiasm and the wife soon has an enormous, room-shaking, screaming orgasm. Smiling, the husband drops the towel, taps the young man on the shoulder and says to him triumphantly, 'THAT'S how you wave a f***ing towel, sonny!'

GENERAL SMUT

———————— Original Message ————————

From: willis
To: webbo
Sent: Thursday, April 03, 2003 9:21 PM
Subject: FW: The object of sex

'I believe that sex is one of the most beautiful, natural, wholesome things that money can buy.'
US author Tom Clancy

'There are a number of mechanical devices that increase sexual arousal, particularly in women. Chief among these is the Mercedes Benz 380 SL.'
US author Lynn Lavner

'According to a new survey, women say they feel more comfortable undressing in front of men than they do undressing in front of other women. They say that women are too judgemental, where, of course, men are just grateful.'
US actor Robert De Niro

'You know "that look" women get when they want sex? Me neither.'
US actor-comedian Steve Martin

'Women need a reason to have sex. Men just need a place.'
US actor-comedian Billy Crystal

'Ah, yes, divorce, from the Latin word meaning to rip out a man's genitals through his wallet.'
US actor-comedian Robin Williams

'Instead of getting married again, I'm going to find a woman I don't like and just give her a house.'
British rock star Rod Stewart

'Having sex is like playing bridge. If you don't have a good partner, you'd better have a good hand.'
US movie actor, comedian and director Woody Allen

'Bisexuality immediately doubles your chances for a date on Saturday night.'
US actor-comedian Rodney Dangerfield

'My girlfriend always laughs during sex, no matter what she's reading.'
Apple Computers founder Steve Jobs

'There's very little advice in men's magazines, because men think, "I know what I'm doing. Just show me somebody naked."'
US comedian Jerry Seinfeld

GENERAL SMUT

'There's a new medical crisis. Doctors are reporting that many men are having allergic reactions to latex condoms. They say they cause severe swelling. So what's the problem?'
US actor Dustin Hoffman

'See, the problem is that God gives men a brain and a penis, and only enough blood to run one at a time.'
US actor-comedian Robin Williams

THE WORLD'S GREATEST EMAIL JOKE BOOK

---------- Original Message ----------

From: willis
To: webbo
Sent: Wednesday, March 26, 2003 11:04 AM
Subject: FW: Sugar daddy

A girl goes to see her mother and tells her that she has missed her period for two months. Very worried, the mother goes to the chemist and buys a pregnancy testing kit. The test gives a positive result. Shouting, cursing and crying, the mother asks, 'Who was the pig that did this to you? I want to know!' Her daughter picks up the phone and makes a call.

Half an hour later a new Ferrari pulls up outside the house. A mature and distinguished man, with grey hair and impeccably dressed in a very expensive suit, steps out of it and enters the house. He sits in the living room with the father, mother and daughter, and tells them, 'Good morning, your daughter has informed me of the problem. I can't marry her because of my personal family situation, but I will take responsibility. If a girl is born I will bequeath her three shops, two townhouses, a beach villa and a £500,000 bank account. If a boy is born, my legacy will be a couple of factories and a £500,000 bank account. If it is twins, I'll leave a factory and £250,000 each. However, if there is a miscarriage...'

GENERAL SMUT

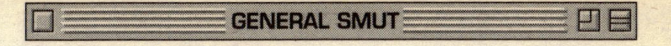

At this point, the father, who had remained silent all the time, places a hand firmly on the man's shoulder and tells him, 'You'll f**k her again!'

THE WORLD'S GREATEST EMAIL JOKE BOOK

---------- Original Message ----------

From: willis
To: webbo
Sent: Tuesday, March 25, 2003 10:50 PM
Subject: Sexual harrassment

Each day, a man walks up to a woman in his office, stands very close to her, draws in a large breath of air and tells her that her hair smells nice. After a week of this the woman can't stand it any longer and goes to Human Resources. Without identifying the man, she describes what the co-worker does and explains that she wants to file a sexual harassment suit against him. The HR supervisor is puzzled by this approach, and asks, 'What's sexually threatening about a co-worker telling you your hair smells nice?'

The woman replies, 'It's Keith, the midget.'

GENERAL SMUT

---— Original Message ———

From: webbo
To: willis
Sent: Monday, February 05, 2001 11:42 AM
Subject: Bond chat-up line

A rather confident agent 007 walks into a bar and takes a seat next to a very attractive woman. He gives her a quick glance, then casually looks at his watch for a moment. The woman notices this and asks, 'Is your date running late?'

'No,' he replies. 'I've just been given this state-of-the-art watch and I was just testing it.'

'A state-of-the-art watch?' says the intrigued woman. 'What's so special about it?'

'It uses alpha waves to talk to me telepathically,' he explains.

'What is it telling you now?'

'Well, it says you're not wearing any knickers…'

The woman giggles and replies, 'Well, it must be broken because I am wearing knickers!'

Bond tut-tuts, taps his watch and says, 'Damn thing must be an hour fast.'

THE WORLD'S GREATEST EMAIL JOKE BOOK

———————— Original Message ————————

From: willis
To: webbo
Sent: Thursday, July 12, 2001 5:18 PM
Subject: FW: Gentlemen's quiz

1. **In the company of feminists, having sex should be referred to as:**
a) Love making
b) Screwing
c) The pigskin bus pulling into tuna town

2. **You should make love to a woman for the first time only after you've both shared:**
a) Your views about what you expect from a sexual relationship
b) Your blood-test results
c) Five tequila slammers

3. **You time your orgasm so that:**
a) Your partner climaxes first
b) You both climax simultaneously
c) You don't miss *Match of the Day*

4. **Passionate, spontaneous sex on the kitchen floor is:**
a) Healthy, creative love play
b) Not the sort of thing your wife/girlfriend would ever agree to

GENERAL SMUT

c) Not the sort of thing your wife/girlfriend need ever find out about

5. Spending the whole night cuddling a woman you've just had sex with is:
a) The best part of the experience
b) The second best part of the experience
c) £50 extra

6. Your girlfriend says she's gained 2kg in weight in the last month. You tell her that it is:
a) Not a concern of yours
b) Not a problem – she can join your gym
c) A conservative estimate

7. You think today's 'sensitive man' is:
a) A myth
b) An oxymoron
c) A moron

8. Foreplay is to sex what an:
a) An appetiser is to an entrée
b) Priming is to painting
c) A queue is to an amusement-park ride

THE WORLD'S GREATEST EMAIL JOKE BOOK

9. Which of the following are you most likely to find yourself saying at the end of a relationship?
a) 'I hope we can still be friends.'
b) 'I'm not in right now. Please leave a message after the tone…'
c) 'Welcome to Dumpsville. Population: you.'

10. A woman who is uncomfortable watching you masturbate:
a) Probably needs a little more time before she can cope with that sort of intimacy
b) Is uptight and a waste of time
c) Shouldn't have sat next to you on the bus in the first place

If you answered 'a' more than seven times, check your pants to make sure you really are a man. If you answered 'b' more than seven times, check into therapy – you're still a little confused. If you answered 'c' more than seven times, give me a call. Let's go drinking.

GENERAL SMUT

---— Original Message ———

From: webbo
To: willis
Sent: Wednesday, October 18, 2000 10:07 AM
Subject: FW: Surgery

After her fifth child, Lucy decided that she should have some cosmetic surgery 'down below' to restore herself to her former youthful glory – her gammon was dangling a bit too low and looked like a ripped-out fireplace. Time and childbirth had taken its toll and she reckoned that, with five children now being the limit, she'd tidy things up with a nip here and a tuck there so it looked more like a Cornish pasty rather than toad in the hole.

Following the operation Lucy awoke from her anaesthetic to find three roses at the end of the bed. 'Who are these from?' she asked the nurse. 'They're very nice but I'm a bit confused as to why I've received them.'
'Well,' said the nurse, 'the first is from the surgeon. The operation went so well and you were such a model patient that he wanted to say thanks.'
'Ah, that's really nice' said Lucy.
'The second is from your husband. He's delighted the operation was such a success that he can't wait to get you home. Apparently it'll be the first time he's touched the sides for years and he's very excited!'

'Brilliant!' said Lucy. 'And the third?'
'That's from Eric in the burns unit,' said the nurse. 'He just wanted to say thanks for his new ears.'

---------------------- Original Message ----------------------

```
From: willis
To: webbo
Sent: Tuesday, May 08, 2001 9:23 PM
Subject: Fwd: Boots
```

A lady goes into a bar and sees a cowboy with his feet propped up on a table. He has the biggest feet she's ever seen. The woman asks the cowboy if it's true what they say about men with big feet. The cowboy says, 'Sure is. Why don't you come back to my place and let me prove it?'

The woman thinks why not and spends the night with him. The next day she hands the cowboy a $100 bill. Blushing he says, 'I'm flattered. Nobody has ever paid me for my services before.'

'Well don't be,' replies the woman. 'Take this money and buy some boots that fit!'

GENERAL SMUT

---- Original Message ----

From: willis
To: webbo
Sent: Wednesday, January 24, 2001 10:33 AM
Subject: FW: The first time

A girl invites her boyfriend to her house, one Friday night, to have dinner with her parents. This being a big event, the girl tells her boyfriend that after dinner she would like to go out and 'do it' for the first time.

The boy is ecstatic, but he has never done it before, so he takes a trip to the pharmacy to get some protection. The pharmacist helps the boy for about an hour. He tells the boy everything there is to know about doing it and using protection. At the till, the pharmacist asks the boy how many condoms he'd like to buy — a 3 pack, a 10 pack or a family pack. The boy insists on the family pack because he thinks he will be very busy, it being his first time.

That night, the boy arrives at his girlfriend's house and meets her at the door. 'Oh, I'm so excited for you to meet my parents,' she says. 'Come in.'
The boy goes inside and is taken to the dinner table, where the girl's parents are seated. The boy quickly offers to say grace and bows his head. A minute passes and the boy is still deep in prayer, with his head down. Ten minutes pass and still there is no movement from

the boy. Finally, after 20 minutes with his head down, the girlfriend leans over and whispers, 'I had no idea you were so religious.'

The boy turns and whispers back, 'I had no idea your father was a pharmacist.'

---------- Original Message ----------

From: webbo
To: willis
Sent: Wednesday, January 17, 2001 6:29 PM
Subject: Jack

An executive was in a quandary. He had to get rid of one of his staff and had narrowed it down to one of two people, Debra or Jack. It would be a hard decision to make, as they were equally qualified and both did excellent work. He finally decided that, in the morning, whichever one used the water cooler first would have to go. Debra came in the next morning, hugely hungover after partying all night. She went to the cooler to get some water so she could take an aspirin. The executive approached her and said, 'Debra, I've never done this before, but I have to lay you or Jack off.'
'Could you jack off?' Debra replied. 'I have a terrible headache.'

GENERAL SMUT

———————— Original Message ————————

From: webbo
To: willis
Sent: Tuesday, June 24, 2003 10:26 PM
Subject: Hotel service

While passing by a phone box, a man staying at a nearby hotel sees a card offering sexual services and decides to remove it. Back at the hotel he rings the number and a lady with a silky soft voice asks if she can be of assistance. The man explains he would like a blow job and a regular and a doggie, plus some bondage and finishing with a pearl necklace. 'What do you think?' he asks.

'That sounds really good,' says the lady, 'but if you press 9 first you'll get an outside line.'

THE WORLD'S GREATEST EMAIL JOKE BOOK

———————— Original Message ————————

From: willis
To: webbo
Sent: Wednesday, July 10, 2002 10:43 PM
Subject: 10-speed bike

Johnny asked for a 10-speed bicycle. His father replied, 'Son, we'd love to give you one, but the mortgage on this house is £80,000, so there's no way we can afford it.'

The next day the father saw little Johnny heading out of the door with a suitcase. 'Son, where are you going?' he asked.

'I was walking past your room last night and I heard you tell Mum you were pulling out,' said little Johnny, 'I heard her tell you to wait because she was coming too. And I'll be f***ed if I'm sticking around here by myself with an £80,000 mortgage and no means of transportation.'

GENERAL SMUT

———————— Original Message ————————

From: willis
To: webbo
Sent: Thursday, July 03, 2003 11:08 PM
Subject: Viagra

A man walks into a pharmacy and says to the pharmacist, 'Listen, I have three girls coming over tonight. I've never had three girls all at once. I need something to keep me horny, keep me potent.'

The pharmacist reaches under the counter, unlocks the bottom drawer and takes out a small cardboard box marked with the label 'Viagra Extra Strength'. 'Here,' he says. 'If you eat this, you'll go nuts for 12 hours.'
'Great, give me three boxes,' says the man.

The next day he returns to the pharmacy, limps up to the pharmacist and pulls down his pants. The pharmacist looks in horror at the man's penis, which is black and blue, with skin hanging off in places. In a pained voice, the man moans out, 'Give me some Deep Heat!'
'You can't put Deep Heat on that!' exclaims the pharmacist.
'No, it's for my arms,' says the man. 'The girls didn't show up.'

THE WORLD'S GREATEST EMAIL JOKE BOOK

---------- Original Message ----------

```
From: webbo
To: willis
Sent: Wednesday, September 24, 2003 2:33 PM
Subject: FW: Birthday
```

Two weeks ago it was my 30th birthday and I wasn't feeling too good that morning. I went to breakfast knowing my wife would be pleasant and say 'happy birthday' and probably have a present for me. As it turned out, she didn't even say 'good morning', let alone 'happy birthday'. I thought, well, that's wives for you... The children will remember. The children came in to breakfast and didn't say a word. So when I left for work I was feeling low and despondent.

As I walked into my office, my secretary Janet said, 'Good morning, Boss. Happy birthday!' And I felt a little better that someone had remembered. I worked until noon, then Janet knocked on my door and said, 'You know, it's such a beautiful day outside, and it's your birthday — let's go out to lunch.'
'Wow,' I said, 'that's the greatest thing I've heard all day. Let's go!'

Instead of going to our usual lunch place, we went to a private little restaurant. We had two Martinis and enjoyed our food tremendously. On the way back to the office, she said, 'You know, it's such a beautiful day.

GENERAL SMUT

We don't need to go back to the office, do we?'
'No, I guess not,' I agreed.
'Let's go to my flat,' she suggested.

After arriving at her flat she said, 'Boss, if you don't mind, I think I'll go into the bedroom and slip into something more comfortable.'
'Of course!' I excitedly replied.

She went into the bedroom and in about six minutes came out carrying a huge birthday cake followed by my wife, children and dozens of our friends, all singing 'Happy Birthday'. And I just sat there on the couch, naked.

THE WORLD'S GREATEST EMAIL JOKE BOOK

———————— Original Message ————————

```
From: willis
To: webbo
Sent: Friday, July 28, 2000 10:51 AM
Subject: FW: Worm in a hole
```

A little boy and his grandfather are raking leaves in the garden. The little boy finds an earthworm trying to get back into its hole. 'Grandpa, I bet I can put that worm back in that hole,' he says.

'I'll bet you £5 you can't,' replies the grandfather. 'It's too wiggly and limp to put back in that little hole.'

The little boy runs into the house and comes back out with a bottle of hairspray. He sprays the worm until it is straight and stiff as a board. Then he puts the worm back into the hole.

The grandfather hands the little boy £5, grabs the hairspray and runs into the house. Thirty minutes later he comes back out and hands the little boy another £5. 'Grandpa, you already gave me five pounds,' says the boy.
'I know,' says the grandfather. 'That's from your grandma.'

GENERAL SMUT

---— Original Message ———

From: willis
To: webbo
Sent: Friday, July 28, 2000 10:51 AM
Subject: FW: Elephant trunk

A man gets his penis severed in a car accident. When he wakes up in the hospital, he rings for the doctor. The doctor comes in and tells him what happened.
'So what are my options?' asks the patient.
'You have two options. We can sew your penis back on, but it will cost you about £500,000. Or we can sew on a baby elephant's trunk. It will look a bit different, but it will feel the same and that will only cost about £500.'
'Well, I'm low on cash so I'll have to go with the elephant trunk,' says the man.

About two weeks later, the man is out to dinner with friends when all of a sudden the trunk comes up from under the table, grabs a biscuit, then returns back under the table. 'God, I hope nobody saw that!' thinks the man to himself.

About five minutes later, the trunk comes up and grabs another biscuit. This time the man's friends see it. 'My God! What on earth was that?' they ask. So the man tells them the story of the accident and the surgery.
'Wow, that's amazing!' they exclaim. 'Can you do that again?'

THE WORLD'S GREATEST EMAIL JOKE BOOK

'Well, I probably could,' says the man, 'but I don't think my arse could take another biscuit!'

---——————— Original Message ———————

From: willis
To: webbo
Sent: Friday, July 28, 2000 10:51 AM
Subject: FW: Chastity test

King Arthur was preparing to go on an expedition, which meant he would be away from Camelot for an indefinite period of time. The King was worried about leaving Queen Guinevere alone with all those horny Knights of the Round Table. So he went to Merlin for some advice. After explaining his predicament to Merlin, the wizard looked thoughtful. He told the King that he would try to come up with a solution and asked him to come back in a week. A week later, King Arthur was back in Merlin's laboratory, where the good wizard was showing him his latest invention. It was a chastity belt, except that it had a rather large hole in the most obvious place.

'This is no good, Merlin!' the King exclaimed. 'Look at this opening. How is this supposed to protect the Queen?'

'Ah, sire, just observe,' said Merlin as he searched his

GENERAL SMUT

cluttered workbench until he found what he was looking for. He then selected his most worn-out wand, one that he was going to discard anyway, and inserted it in the gaping aperture of the chastity belt, whereupon a small guillotine blade came down and cut it neatly in two.

'Merlin, you are a genius!' cried the grateful monarch. 'Now I can leave, knowing that my Queen is fully protected.'

After putting Guinevere in the device, King Arthur set out upon his quest. Several years passed until he returned to Camelot. Immediately he assembled all his knights in the courtyard and had them drop their trousers for an informal 'short arm' inspection. Sure enough, each one of them was either amputated or damaged in some way – except for Sir Galahad.

'Sir Galahad!' exclaimed King Arthur. 'The one and only true knight! Only you among all the nobles have been true to me. What is it in my power to grant you? Name it and it is yours!' But Sir Galahad was speechless.

THE WORLD'S GREATEST EMAIL JOKE BOOK

———————— Original Message ————————

From: willis
To: webbo
Sent: Friday, July 28, 2000 10:51 AM
Subject: FW: Duck test

A game warden came upon a duck hunter who had bagged three ducks, and decided to 'enforce the laws pending'. He stopped the hunter, flashed his badge and said, 'Looks like you've had a pretty good day. Mind if I inspect your kill?'

The hunter shrugged and handed the ducks to the warden. The warden took one of the ducks, inserted his finger into the duck's rectum, pulled it out, sniffed it and said, 'This here's a Washington State duck. Do you have a Washington State hunting licence?' The hunter pulled out his wallet and calmly showed the warden a Washington State hunting licence. The warden took the second duck, inserted his finger in the bird's rectum, pulled it out, sniffed it and said, 'This here's an Idaho duck. Do you have an Idaho State hunting licence?' The hunter, a bit put out, produced an Idaho State hunting licence. The warden took the third duck, conducted the same finger test and said, 'This here's an Oregon State duck. Do you have an Oregon State hunting licence?' Once again, only this time more aggravated, the hunter produced the appropriate licence.

GENERAL SMUT

The warden, a little miffed at being unsuccessful, handed the ducks back to the hunter and said, 'You've got all of these licences – just where the heck are you from?'
The hunter dropped his pants, bent over and said, 'You're so smart, YOU tell ME!'

——————— Original Message ———————

From: willis
To: webbo
Sent: Monday, September 25, 2000 5:00 PM
Subject: FW: The car with everything

While on a golf tour in Ireland, Tiger Woods drives his Volvo into a petrol station in Cork. The attendant greets him in a typical Cork manner, unaware of who the golf pro is. 'Top of the mornin' to yez, sir,' he says.

Tiger Woods nods a quick 'hello' and bends forward to pick up the pump. As he does so, two tees fall out of his top pocket on to the ground.
'What are dey, son?' says the attendant.
'They're called tees,' replies Tiger.
'What're dey for?' enquires the Cork man.
'They're for putting my balls on while I'm driving,' says Tiger.
'Jaysus,' says the Cork man. 'Dem boys at Volvo tink of feckin' everyting!'

THE WORLD'S GREATEST EMAIL JOKE BOOK

---------- Original Message ----------

From: willis
To: webbo
Sent: Thursday, September 14, 2000 10:33 AM
Subject: Old couple's secret

An old couple are reminiscing about their life together one evening. 'Do you remember the first time we had sex, over 50 years ago?' says the old man. 'We went behind the bar, and you leaned against the fence while I made love to you from behind.'
'Yes,' replies his wife, 'I remember it well.'
'OK,' the old man continues, 'how about taking a stroll round there again and we can do it for old times' sake?'
'Ooh, Henry, you devil! That sounds like a great idea,' she answers.

A man sitting at the next table is listening to all this and having a chuckle to himself. He thinks, 'I've got to see this, two old-timers having sex against a fence.' So he follows them.

They walk along haltingly, leaning on each other for support and aided by walking sticks. Finally they get to the back of the bar and make their way to the fence. The old lady lifts her skirt and takes down her knickers, and the old man drops his trousers. She turns around and, as she hangs on to the fence, the old man moves

GENERAL SMUT

in. Suddenly they erupt into the most furious sex the watching man has ever seen, bucking and jumping like 18-year-olds. This goes on for about 40 minutes. She's yelling, 'Ohhh God!' He's hanging on to her hips for dear life. It's the most athletic sex imaginable. Finally they both collapse, panting, on the ground.

The watching man is amazed. He thinks he has learned something about life that he didn't know before. He starts to think about his own aged parents and wonders whether they still have sex like this.

After about half an hour of lying on the ground, recovering, the old couple struggle to their feet and put their clothes back on. The man, still watching, thinks, 'That was truly amazing. He was going like a train. I've got to ask him what his secret is.' As the couple pass by, the man says to them, 'That was something else. You must have been shagging for about 40 minutes. How do you manage it? Is there some sort of secret?'

'No, there's no secret,' says the old man. 'Except 50 years ago that damn fence wasn't electric.'

THE WORLD'S GREATEST EMAIL JOKE BOOK

---––––––––––––––––– Original Message ––––––––––––––––-

From: webbo
To: willis
Sent: Wednesday, November 08, 2000 5:53 PM
Subject: Stuff

Q. Why do they call it PMS?
A. Because Mad Cow Disease was already taken.

Q. What's the difference between a muff-dive and a speedtrap?
A. With a muff-dive you always have a clear view of the c**t!

Q. How do you know when you are getting old?
A. When you start having dry dreams and wet farts.

Q. Why would a bloke give his wife a pair of slippers and a dildo for her birthday?
A. Because if she doesn't like the slippers she can go and get f**ked.

Q. What's the difference between a police car and a pair of knickers?
A. You can only fit one c**t in a pair of knickers.

Q. When is a pixie not a pixie?
A. When he's got his head up a fairy's skirt – then he's a goblin'.

GENERAL SMUT

Q. What's the definition of a Yankee?
A. Same thing as a 'quickie', only you do it yourself!

Q. What's the difference between a blonde and a broom cupboard?
A. Only two men can fit inside a broom cupboard at once.

Q. Why do blondes have more fun?
A. They are easier to keep amused.

Q. Did you hear about the new shoe Nike is making for lesbians?
A. The tongue is twice as long and it will only need one finger to get it off.

Q. How do you tell that you have a high sperm count?
A. Your date has to chew before she swallows.

THE WORLD'S GREATEST EMAIL JOKE BOOK

―――――――― Original Message ――――――――

From: willis
To: webbo
Sent: Friday, November 10, 2000 1:18 AM
Subject: Phone call

'Hello,' says a little girl's voice.
'Hi, love, it's Daddy,' says Bob. 'Is Mummy near the phone?'
'No, Daddy. She's upstairs in the bedroom with Uncle Frank.'
After a brief pause, Bob says, 'But you haven't got an Uncle Frank, love!'
'Yes, I do, and he's upstairs in the bedroom with Mummy!'
'OK, then. Here's what I want you to do. Put down the phone, run upstairs, knock on the bedroom door and shout to Mummy and Uncle Frank that my car's just pulled up outside the house.'
'OK, Daddy!'
A few minutes later, the little girl comes back to the phone. 'I did what you said, Daddy.'
'And what happened?'
'Well, Mummy jumped out of bed with no clothes on and ran around screaming. Then she tripped over the rug and fell down the front steps and she's just lying there. Her neck is at a funny angle. I think she's dead.'
'Oh my God... And what about Uncle Frank?'
'He jumped out of bed with no clothes on too, and he

was all scared, and he jumped out of the back window into the swimming pool. But he must have forgotten that last week you took out all the water to clean it, so he hit the bottom and he's just lying there, not moving. He may be dead too.'

There is a long pause, then Bob says, 'Swimming pool? Is this 8547039?'

THE WORLD'S GREATEST EMAIL JOKE BOOK

──────── Original Message ────────

From: willis
To: webbo
Sent: Tuesday, January 23, 2001 11:40 AM
Subject: FW: Farmer's favour

One day a farmer was in town picking up supplies. He stopped by the hardware shop and picked up a bucket and an anvil. Then he stopped by the livestock dealer to buy a couple of chickens and a goose. 'Now I have a problem,' he said. 'How will I carry all this stuff home?'

The livestock dealer said, 'Why don't you put the anvil in the bucket, carry the bucket in one hand, put a chicken under each arm and carry the goose in your other hand?'

'Hey, thanks!' said the farmer, and off he went. While he was walking he met a little old lady who told him she was lost. 'Can you tell me how to get to 150 Mockingbird Lane?' she asked.

'Well, as a matter of fact,' said the farmer, 'I live at 160 Mockingbird Lane. Let's take my short cut and go down this alley. We'll be there in no time.'

'But how do I know that when we get in the alley you won't hold me up against the wall, pull up my skirt and ravish me?' said the little old lady.

'For heaven's sake, lady!' said the farmer. 'I'm carrying a bucket, an anvil, two chickens and a goose. How in the world could I possibly hold you up against the wall and do that?'

GENERAL SMUT

'Set the goose down, cover him with the bucket, put the anvil on top of the bucket – and I'll hold the chickens.'

---——————— Original Message ———————

From: webbo
To: willis
Sent: Tuesday, September 26, 2000 10:29 AM
Subject: FW: Dirty Disney

Pinocchio had a human girlfriend, who would sometimes complain about splinters when they were having sex. So Pinocchio went to visit Gepetto to see if he could help. Gepetto suggested that he try a little sandpaper, wherever indicated, and Pinocchio skipped away enlightened.
A couple of weeks later, Gepetto saw Pinocchio bouncing happily through town and asked him, 'How's the girlfriend?'
'Who needs a girlfriend?' Pinocchio replied.

Mickey Mouse and Minnie Mouse were in a divorce court and the judge said to Mickey, 'You say here that your wife is crazy.'
'I didn't say she was crazy,' replied Mickey. 'I said she's f**king Goofy.'

THE WORLD'S GREATEST EMAIL JOKE BOOK

———————— Original Message ————————

From: webbo
To: willis
Sent: Tuesday, April 24, 2001 11:13 AM
Subject: FW: Ghosts

A professor at the University of Kentucky is giving a lecture on the supernatural. To get a feel for his audience, he asks, 'How many people here believe in ghosts?' About 90 students raise their hands. 'Well that's a good start. Out of those of you who believe in ghosts, do any of you think you've ever seen a ghost?' About 40 students raise their hands. 'That's really good,' says the professor. 'I'm really glad you take this seriously. Has anyone here ever talked to a ghost?' Fifteen students raise their hands. 'That's a great response. Has anyone here ever touched a ghost?' Three students raise their hands. 'That's fantastic. But let me ask you one more question: have any of you ever made love to a ghost?' One student way at the back raises his hand. The professor is astonished. He takes off his glasses, takes a step back and says, 'Son, in all the years I've been giving this lecture, no one has ever claimed to have slept with a ghost. You've got to come up here and tell us about your experience.'

The redneck student replies with a nod and a grin, and begins to make his way up to the podium. As the student ambles slowly towards the podium the professor says, 'Well, tell us what it's like to have sex with a ghost.'

GENERAL SMUT

'Ghost?!' replies the student. 'Shiiit… From way back there I thought you said 'goats'.'

———————— Original Message ————————

From: webbo
To: willis
Sent: Wednesday, February 26, 2003 12:17 PM
Subject: FW: Some of the finest double entendres

'They seem cold out there. They're rubbing each other and he's only come in his shorts.'

TV correspondent Michael Buerk, watching presenter Phillipa Forrester cuddle up to a male astronomer for warmth during BBC1's UK eclipse coverage

'Some weeks Nick likes to use Fanny, other weeks he prefers to do it by himself.'

BBC sports commentator Ken Brown, remarking on golfer Nick Faldo and his caddie Fanny Sunneson lining up shots at the Scottish Open

'Stephen Hendry jumps on Steve Davis's misses every chance he gets.'

Sports commentator Mike Hallett, discussing missed snooker shots on Sky Sports

THE WORLD'S GREATEST EMAIL JOKE BOOK

'Colin had a hard on in practice earlier, and I bet he wished he had a hard on now.'
Sports commentator Jack Burnicle, talking about Colin Edwards's tyre choice on Eurosport's World Superbikes

'She was practising "fastest finger first" by herself in bed last night.'
TV presenter Chris Tarrant, discussing the first *Who Wants to Be a Millionaire* winner Judith Keppel on ITV show *This Morning*

'Tony has a quick look between his legs and likes what he sees.'
Sky Sport's *The Winning* Post reporter Stewart Machin, commentating on jockey Tony McCoy's formidable lead

'Well, Phil, tell us about your amazing third leg.'
TV sports commentator Ross King, discussing relays with champion runner Phil Redmond

'With his lovely soft hands he just tossed it off.'
Commentator Bobby Simpson, observing English cricketer Neil Fairbrother hit a single during a Durham v Lancashire match

'There's nothing like a big hot sausage inside you on a cold night like this.'
BBC TV presenter Clair Frisby, talking about a jumbo hot dog on *Look North*

GENERAL SMUT

'What does it feel like being rammed up the backside by Barrichello?'

Sports commentator James Allen, interviewing Ralf Schumacher at a Grand Prix

'Ballesteros felt much better today after a 69.'

Sports commentator Steve Ryder, covering the US Masters Golf Championship

'My word,' he said, 'look at that magnificent erection.'

Commentator and ex-jockey Brough Scott, remarking on the new stand at Doncaster racecourse

'They usually have four or five dreams a night about coming from different positions.'

Ex-jockey and TV presenter Willie Carson, explaining to his colleague Claire Balding how jockeys prepare for a big race

'You'd eat beaver if you could get it.'

Presenter Carenza Lewis, speaking about finding food in the Middle Ages on Channel 4's Time Team Live

'So, Bob, where's that eight inches you promised me last night?'

A female news anchor, questioning the weatherman the day after it was supposed to have snowed, but didn't. Not only did he have to leave the set, but half the crew did too, they were laughing so hard.

THE WORLD'S GREATEST EMAIL JOKE BOOK

'One of the reasons Arnie [Arnold Palmer] is playing so well is that, before each tee shot, his wife takes out his balls and kisses them... Oh my God! What have I just said?!'
US PGA Golf Championship commentator

'Julian Dicks is everywhere. It's like they've got 11 Dicks on the field.'
Football commentator on Metro Radio

'Ah, isn't that nice? The wife of the Cambridge president is kissing the cox of the Oxford crew.'
BBC sports commentator Harry Carpenter at the 1977 Oxford - Cambridge boat race

'This is really a lovely horse. I once rode her mother.'
Horse-racing commentator Ted Walsh

'Andrew Mehrtens loves it when Daryl Gibson comes inside of him.'
New Zealand rugby commentator

'And this is Gregoriava from Bulgaria. I saw her snatch this morning and it was amazing!'
Weightlifting commentator Pat Glenn

| **GENERAL SMUT** |

———————— Original Message ————————

From: webbo
To: willis
Sent: Saturday, February 10, 2001 5:33 PM
Subject: FW: Clarification

Q. What do you call a Serbian prostitute?
A. Sloberdown Mycockyoubitch.

Q. What's a mixed feeling?
A. When you see your mother-in-law backing off a cliff in your new car.

Q. What's the height of conceit?
A. Having an orgasm and calling out your own name.

Q. What's the definition of macho?
A. Jogging home from your own vasectomy.

Q. What is the difference between a drug dealer and a hooker?
A. A hooker can wash her crack and sell it again.

Q. What's the difference between a G-spot and a golf ball?
A. A man will actually search for a golf ball.

Q. How can you recognise a porno star at a petrol station?
A. Just as the petrol starts up the hose, he pulls out the nozzle and sprays petrol all over the car.

Q. How do New Zealanders practise safe sex?
A. They spray-paint Xs on the back of the animals that kick.

Q. Why is divorce so expensive?
A. Because it's worth it.

Q. What do Tupperware and a walrus have in common?
A. They both like a tight seal.

Q. What do a Christmas tree and a priest have in common?
A. Their balls are just for decoration.

Q. What is the difference between 'Oooh' and 'Aaah'?
A. About 10cm.

Q. What do you call a lesbian with fat fingers?
A. Well hung.

Q. Why do gay men wear ribbed condoms?
A. For traction in the mud.

Q. What's the difference between purple and pink?
A. The grip.

GENERAL SMUT

Q. How do you find a blind man in a nudist colony?
A. It's not hard.

Q. How do you circumcise a hillbilly?
A. Kick his sister in the jaw.

Q. What's the difference between a girlfriend and a wife?
A. 20kg.

Q. What's the difference between a boyfriend and a husband?
A. 45 minutes.

Q. Why do men find it difficult to make eye contact?
A. Breasts don't have eyes.

Q. What is the difference between medium and rare?
A. Fifteen centimetres is medium, 20cm is rare.

Q. Why don't men fake orgasm?
A. Cos no man would pull those faces on purpose.

Q. Why do most women pay more attention to their appearance than to improving their minds?
A. Because most men are stupid but few are blind.

Q. Why do women rub their eyes when they get up in the morning?
A. They don't have balls to scratch.

| **GENERAL SMUT** |

---------- Original Message ----------

From: willis
To: webbo
Sent: Thursday, October 09, 2003 4:55 PM
Subject: FW: Gorilla charm

A small West Virginia wild animal park had acquired a very rare species of gorilla. Within a few weeks, the female gorilla became very horny and difficult to handle. Upon examination, the park veterinarian determined the problem: the gorilla was in heat. To make matters worse, there were no male gorillas of her species available.

While reflecting on their problem, the park administrators noticed Ed, a part-time redneck intern, responsible for cleaning the animals' cages. Ed, like most rednecks, had little sense, but possessed ample ability to satisfy a female of ANY species. So the park administrators thought they might have a solution. Ed was approached with a proposition: would he be willing to have sex with the gorilla for $500?

Ed showed some interest, but said he would have to think the matter over carefully. The following day, Ed announced that he would accept their offer, but only under three conditions. 'First,' he said, 'I don't want to have to kiss the gorilla. Second, you must never tell anyone about this.' The park administrators quickly agreed to these conditions, so they asked what was his third condition. 'You gotta give me another week to come up with the $500,' he stated.

| **GENERAL SMUT** |

──────── Original Message ────────

From: willis
To: webbo
Sent: Friday, November 28, 2003 9:32 AM
Subject: Dwarf

A dwarf with a lisp goes into a stud farm.
'I'd like to buy a horth,' he says to the owner of the farm.
'What sort of horse?' asks the owner.
'A female horth,' the dwarf replies. So the owner shows him a mare.
'Nithe horth,' says the dwarf. 'Can I thee her eyeth?' So the owner picks up the dwarf to show him the horse's eyes.
'Nithe eyeth,' says the dwarf. 'Can I thee her teeth?' Again the owner picks up the dwarf to show him the horse's teeth.
'Nithe teeth... Can I see her eerth?' By now the owner is getting a little fed up, but again he picks up the dwarf to show him the horse's ears.
'Nithe eerth,' he says. 'Now, can I see her twot?' With this the owner picks the dwarf up by the scruff of his neck and shoves his head deep inside the horse's vagina. He holds him there for a couple of seconds before pulling him out and putting him down.

The dwarf shakes his head and says, 'Perhaps I thould rephrathe that... Can I thee her run around?'

🖖 It's A Mad World

———————— Original Message ————————

From: willis
To: webbo
Sent: Thursday, September 26, 2002 9:04 PM
Subject: Only in America

A lawyer in Charlotte, North Carolina, USA, purchased a box of very rare and expensive cigars, then insured them against fire among other things. A month later he had smoked his entire stockpile of these great cigars, but as yet hadn't made his first premium payment on the policy. So the lawyer filed a claim against the insurance company, in which he stated that the cigars were lost 'in a series of small fires'. The insurance company refused to pay, citing the obvious reason: that the man had consumed the cigars in the normal fashion. The lawyer sued and won!

In delivering the ruling the judge agreed with the insurance company that the claim was frivolous. Nevertheless, the judge stated that the lawyer held a policy from the company, in which it had warranted that the cigars were insurable and also guaranteed that it would insure them against fire, without defining what would considered to be 'unacceptable fire', and was obligated to pay the claim.

Rather than endure a lengthy and costly appeal process, the insurance company accepted the ruling and paid $15,000 (£8,000) to the lawyer for his loss of the rare cigars.

Now for the best part... After the lawyer cashed the cheque, the insurance company had him arrested on 24 counts of arson! With his own insurance claim and testimony from the previous case being used against him, the lawyer was convicted of intentionally burning his insured property and was sentenced to 24 months in jail and a $24,000 (£13,000) fine.

This is a true story and was the first-place winner in the recent Criminal Lawyers Award Contest.

IT'S A MAD WORLD

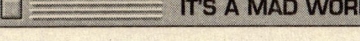

──────── Original Message ────────

```
From: webbo
To: willis
Sent: Tuesday, February 11, 2003 11:45 AM
Subject: FW: Newspaper clippings
```

1. 'Irish police are being handicapped in a search for a stolen van, because they cannot issue a description. It's a special-branch vehicle and they don't want the public to know what it looks like.' (*Guardian*)

2. 'Would the congregation please note that the bowl at the back of the church labelled "for the sick" is for monetary donations only.' (*Churchtown Parish Magazine*)

3. 'There must, for instance, be something very strange in a man who, if left alone in a room with a tea cosy, doesn't try it on.' (*Glasgow Evening News*)

4. 'A young girl who was blown out to sea on a set of inflatable teeth was rescued by a man on an inflatable lobster. A coastguard spokesman commented: "This sort of thing is all too common."' (*The Times*)

5. 'At the height of the gale, the harbour master radioed a coastguard on the spot and asked him to estimate

the wind speed. He replied that he was sorry but he didn't have a gauge. However, if it was any help, the wind had just blown his Land Rover off the cliff.' (*Aberdeen Evening Express*)

6. 'Mrs Irene Graham of Thorpe Avenue, Boscombe, delighted the audience with her reminiscence of the German prisoner of war who was sent each week to do her garden. He was repatriated at the end of 1945. She recalled, "He'd always seemed a nice friendly chap, but when the crocuses came up in the middle of our lawn in February 1946 they spelled out "Heil Hitler".' (*Bournemouth Evening Echo*)

7. 'Commenting on a complaint from a Mr Arthur Purdey about a large gas bill, a spokesman for North West Gas said: "We agree it was rather high for the time of year. It's possible Mr Purdey has been charged for the gas used up during the explosion that blew his house to pieces."' (*Northern Post*)

IT'S A MAD WORLD

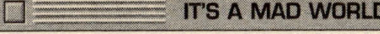

──────── Original Message ────────

From: webbo
To: willis
Sent: Wednesday, April 02, 2003 10:24 AM
Subject: FW: Fantastic behaviour

New York:

Federal investigators have arrested an enigmatic Wall Street whizz on insider-trading charges — and, incredibly, he claims to be a time-traveller from the year 2256!

Sources at the Security and Exchange Commission (SEC) confirm that 44-year-old Andrew Carlssin offered the bizarre explanation for his uncanny success in the stock market after being led off in handcuffs on 28 January. 'We don't believe this guy's story — he's either a lunatic or a pathological liar,' says an SEC insider. 'But the fact is, with an initial investment of only $800 [£400], in two weeks' time he had a portfolio valued at over $350 [£190] million. Every trade he made capitalised on unexpected business developments, which simply can't be pure luck. The only way he could pull it off is with illegal inside information. He's going to sit in a jail cell on Rikers Island until he agrees to give up his sources.'

THE WORLD'S GREATEST EMAIL JOKE BOOK

The past year of nose-diving stock prices has left most investors crying in their beer. So, when Carlssin made a flurry of 126 high-risk trades and came out the winner every time, it raised the eyebrows of Wall Street watchdogs. 'If a company's stock rose due to a merger or technological breakthrough that was supposed to be secret, Mr Carlssin somehow knew about it in advance,' says the SEC source close to the hush-hush, ongoing investigation.

When investigators hauled Carlssin in for questioning, they got more than they bargained for: a mind-boggling four-hour confession. Carlssin declared that he had travelled back in time from over 200 years in the future, when it is common knowledge that our era experienced one of the worst stock plunges in history. Yet anyone armed with knowledge of the handful of stocks destined to go through the roof could make a fortune. 'It was just too tempting to resist,' Carlssin allegedly said in his videotaped confession. 'I had planned to make it look natural, you know, lose a little here and there so it doesn't look too perfect. But I just got caught in the moment.'

In a bid for leniency, Carlssin has reportedly offered to divulge 'historical facts' such as the whereabouts of Osama Bin Laden and a cure for AIDS. All he wants is to be allowed to return to the future in his 'time craft'. However, he refuses to reveal the location of the machine or discuss how it works, supposedly out of fear the technology could 'fall into the wrong hands'.

Officials are quite confident the 'time traveller's' claims are bogus. Yet the SEC source admits, 'No one can find any record of any Andrew Carlssin existing anywhere before December 2002.'

🗔 ≡ THE WORLD'S GREATEST EMAIL JOKE BOOK ≡ 🗂 🗏

---------- Original Message ----------

```
From: webbo
To: willis
Sent: Monday, July 23, 2001 10:39 AM
Subject: FW: One for the clubbers...
```

The following are actual ads that were placed in the Personals section of *Ministry*, the former Ministry of Sound UK clubbing/lifestyle magazine:

ARE YOU AGED 18–30, female, slim build, into hardcore techno, a recent graduate and into politics? Then f**k off! I want a shit-thick 16-year-old bird with no opinions and massive tits! Reply to box ****.

WERE YOU THE girl with braids, blue T-shirt and platform trainers, dancing to left of the stage during JFK's set at Passion last Friday? I was the guy curled up under the speaker stack. I meant to talk to you but I was hallucinating and I thought you had a wolf's head and flippers. But I'm OK now. Reply to box ****.

ATTENTION ALL MAD clubheads in the Toxteth area going to Cream this weekend. Me and my mates are going to nick all your valuables while you're out because we're thieving scally bastards. Reply to ****.

IT'S A MAD WORLD

IF YOU ARE a group of around four House fans in the Acton High Street area of West London and you're particularly into old-skool Chicago sounds, please turn your stereo down because some of us are f**king trying to get some sleep. Reply to ****.

ARE YOU THE tall black-haired guy in the black and silver Versace shirt who I shagged in the Ministry toilets about three months ago without any form of birth control? Please write to me. I'd … ummmm … love to hear from you. Just to see how you are and stuff. Don't worry, there's nothing to worry about. Really. It's just that I'm going to have a … ummm … a PARTY! Yes, that's it. A party. Reply to ****.

WANTED: COCAINE. Lots of it. Reply to ****.

WERE YOU THE man standing three feet away from me at the bar in Fabric, smiling weakly and smelling rather too strongly of Issey Miyake? Because if you look at my tits one more time, I am going to glass you. Reply to ****.

ARE YOU A frequent visitor to the nightclubs of Rugby? They're shite, aren't they? Reply to ****.

THE WORLD'S GREATEST EMAIL JOKE BOOK

———————— Original Message ————————

From: webbo
To: willis
Sent: Tuesday, June 11, 2002 12:00 PM
Subject: FW: Americans know f**k all

Rumsfeld baffles press with 'unknown unknowns'

The United States Defence Secretary, Donald Rumsfeld, has baffled journalists in Brussels by explaining that the greatest threat to Western civilisation may lurk in what he has termed 'unknown unknowns'.

Mr Rumsfeld says he told a meeting of North Atlantic Treaty Organisation (NATO) defence ministers that even US intelligence agencies can often only see the tip of the iceberg when looking for terrorist threats. But this is how he explained it at a media conference:

'There are known knowns,' said Mr Rumsfeld.

'There are things we know that we know. There are known unknowns – that is to say, there are things that we now know we don't know, but there are also unknown unknowns. There are things we do not know we don't know,' said Mr Rumsfeld.

IT'S A MAD WORLD

'So when we do the best we can and we pull all this information together, and we then say well that's basically what we see as the situation, that is really only the known knowns and the known unknowns.

'And each year we discover a few more of those unknown unknowns.'

———————— Original Message ————————

From: webbo
To: willis
Sent: Thursday, July 27, 2000 10:11 AM
Subject: FW: Who's the father?

The following are all replies that have been included on Child Support Agency forms in the section for listing the father's details:

'Regarding the identity of the father of my twins – child A was fathered by [name supplied]. I am unsure as to the identity of the father of child B, but I believe that he was conceived on the same night.'

'I am unsure as to the identity of the father of my child as I was being sick out of a window when taken unexpectedly from behind. I can provide you with a list of names of men that I think were at the party if this helps.'

'I do not know the name of the father of my little girl. She was conceived at a party [address and date supplied], where I had unprotected sex with a man I met that night. I do remember that the sex was so good that I fainted. If you do manage to track down the father can you send me his phone number? Thanks.'

'I don't know the identity of the father of my daughter. He drives a BMW that now has a hole made by my stiletto in one of the door panels. Perhaps you can contact BMW service stations in this area and see if he's had it replaced?'

'I have never had sex with a man. I am awaiting a letter from the Pope confirming that my son's conception was immaculate and that he is Christ risen again.'

'I cannot tell you the name of child A's dad as he informs me that to do so would blow his cover and that would have cataclysmic implications for the British economy. I am torn between doing right by you and right by my country. Please advise.'

IT'S A MAD WORLD

'I do not know who the father of my child was, as all squadies look the same to me. I can confirm that he was a Royal Green Jacket.'

'[Name given] is the father of child A. If you do catch up with him, can you ask him what he did with my AC/DC CDs?'

'From the dates, it seems that my daughter was conceived at Eurodisney. Maybe it really is the Magic Kingdom. So much about that night is a blur.'

'The only thing I remember for sure is that Delia Smith did a programme about eggs earlier in the evening. If I'd have stayed in and watched more TV rather than going to the party at [address supplied], mine might have remained unfertilised.'

THE WORLD'S GREATEST EMAIL JOKE BOOK

---------- Original Message ----------

From: webbo
To: willis
Sent: Wednesday, March 19, 2003 4:44 PM
Subject: FW: The best headlines of 2002

CRACK FOUND ON GOVERNOR'S DAUGHTER

SOMETHING WENT WRONG IN JET CRASH, EXPERT SAYS

POLICE BEGIN CAMPAIGN TO RUN DOWN JAYWALKERS

IRAQI HEAD SEEKS ARMS

IS THERE A RING OF DEBRIS AROUND URANUS?

PROSTITUTES APPEAL TO POPE

PANDA MATING FAILS; VETERINARIAN TAKES OVER

TEACHER STRIKES IDLE KIDS

MINERS REFUSE TO WORK AFTER DEATH

IT'S A MAD WORLD

JUVENILE COURT TO TRY SHOOTING DEFENDANT

WAR DIMS HOPE FOR PEACE

IF STRIKE ISN'T SETTLED QUICKLY, IT MAY LAST A WHILE

COLD WAVE LINKED TO TEMPERATURES

ENFIELD (LONDON) COUPLE SLAIN; POLICE SUSPECT HOMICIDE

RED TAPE HOLDS UP NEW BRIDGES

TYPHOON RIPS THROUGH CEMETERY; HUNDREDS DEAD

MAN STRUCK BY LIGHTNING FACES BATTERY CHARGE

NEW STUDY OF OBESITY LOOKS FOR LARGER TEST GROUP

ASTRONAUT TAKES BLAME FOR GAS IN SPACECRAFT

KIDS MAKE NUTRITIOUS SNACKS

CHEF THROWS HIS HEART INTO HELPING FEED NEEDY

LOCAL HIGH SCHOOL DROPOUTS CUT IN HALF

HOSPITALS ARE SUED BY SEVEN FOOT DOCTORS

───────── Original Message ─────────

From: willis
To: webbo
Sent: Sunday, December 21, 2003 12:48 PM
Subject: FW: Famous insults

'I feel so miserable without you, it's almost like having you here.'
US songwriter Stephen Bishop

'He is a self-made man and worships his creator.'
UK politician John Bright, speaking about his opponent, UK politician Benjamin Disraeli

IT'S A MAD WORLD

'He has all the virtues I dislike and none of the vices I admire.'
Former British Prime Minister Winston Churchill

'A modest little person, with much to be modest about.'
Winston Churchill

'I've just learned about his illness. Let's hope it's nothing trivial.'
US novelist and humorist Irvin S Cobb

'I have never killed a man, but I have read many obituaries with great pleasure.'
US trial lawyer Clarence Darrow

'He has never been known to use a word that might send a reader to the dictionary.'
US writer William Faulkner, speaking about writer Ernest Hemingway

'Poor Faulkner. Does he really think big emotions come from big words?'
Ernest Hemingway, in reply to William Faulkner

'Thank you for sending me a copy of your book; I'll waste no time reading it.'
US writer and educator Moses Hadas

'His ears made him look like a taxicab with both doors open.'
Aviator, film producer, millionaire business man Howard Hughes, speaking about Hollywood film star Clark Gable

'He is not only dull himself, he is the cause of dullness in others.'
English author, critic and lexicographer Samuel Johnson

'He is simply a shiver looking for a spine to run up.'
Former Australian Prime Minister Paul Keating

'He had delusions of adequacy.'
US prize-winning critic Walter Kerr

'There's nothing wrong with you that reincarnation won't cure.'
US comic Jack E Leonard

'He can compress the most words into the smallest idea of any man I know.'
Former US President Abraham Lincoln

'I've had a perfectly wonderful evening. But this wasn't it.'
US actor-comedian Groucho Marx

IT'S A MAD WORLD

'He has the attention span of a lightning bolt.'
US actor, producer and director Robert Redford

'They never open their mouths without subtracting from the sum of human knowledge.'
US legislator and congressman Thomas Brackett Reed

'He inherited some good instincts from his Quaker forebears, but, by diligent hard work, he overcame them.'
US journalist James Reston, speaking about Richard Nixon

'In order to avoid being called a flirt, she always yielded easily.'
French diplomat (Count) Charles Talleyrand

'He loves nature in spite of what it did to him.'
US actor Forrest Tucker

'Why do you sit there looking like an envelope without any address on it?'
US writer Mark Twain

'I didn't attend the funeral, but I sent a nice letter saying I approved of it.'
US writer Mark Twain

'His mother should have thrown him away and kept the stork.'
US actress and writer Mae West

'Some cause happiness wherever they go; others whenever they go.'
Irish dramatist, novelist and poet Oscar Wilde

'He has no enemies, but is intensely disliked by his friends.'
Irish dramatist, novelist and poet Oscar Wilde

'He uses statistics as a drunken man uses lamp-posts… For support rather than illumination.'
Scottish poet and novelist Andrew Lang

'He has Van Gogh's ear for music.'
Austrian-born writer-director Billy Wilder

⇪ Sport

---— Original Message ———

From: willis
To: webbo
Sent: Friday, January 12, 2001 1:13 PM
Subject: FW: Beckham Jokes

THE Manchester United players are in the dressing room on Saturday, just before the game, when Roy Keane walks in. 'Boss,' he says, 'there's a problem. I'm not playing unless I get a cortisone injection.'
'Hey,' says Becks. 'If he's having a new car, so am I.'

*

DAVID Beckham goes shopping, and sees something interesting in the kitchen department of a large department store.

'What's that?' he asks. 'A Thermos flask,' replies the assistant. 'What does it do?' asks Becks. The assistant tells him it keeps hot things hot and cold things cold. Really impressed, Beckham buys one and takes it along to his next training session.

'Here, boys, look at this,' Beckham says proudly. 'It's a Thermos flask.' The lads are impressed. 'What does it do?' they ask. 'It keeps hot things hot and cold things cold,' says David. 'And what have you got in it?' asks Roy Keane.

'Two cups of coffee and a choc ice,' replies David.

*

POSH takes her car into a garage to have some dents removed. The garage man, knowing she isn't the brightest Spice Girl in the world, decides to play a joke on her.
'You don't need me to take those dents out,' he says. 'Just blow up the exhaust pipe and the metal will pop back into place.'

So she takes the car home and tries it. David spots her from the house, opens a window and shouts, 'You daft girl! You have to wind the windows up first!'

SPORT

*

DAVID Beckham is celebrating: '57 days, 57 days!' he shouts happily.
Posh asks him why he is celebrating. He answers: 'Well, I've done this Jigsaw in only 57 days.'
'Is that good?' asks Posh. 'You bet,' says David. 'It says 3 to 5 years on the box.'

*

POSH and Becks are travelling back from Heathrow Airport to Central London.
'Where have you been?' asks the cabbie. 'New York,' says Beckham. 'We saw a show and did some shopping.' 'Did you have any nice meals?' asks the cabbie. 'Yes, one really great one.'

'What was the name of the restaurant?' asks the cabbie. 'Dunno. I can't remember. Name some big railway stations in London,' says Beckham.
The cabbie begins, 'Waterloo, Paddington, Victoria...'
Beckham interrupts excitedly: 'That's it! Victoria, what was the name of that restaurant we went to?'

*

Q: What would David Beckham's name be if he were a Spice Girl?
A: Waste of Spice.

Q: What would England achieve with 11 David Beckhams?
A: An average IQ.

Q: What is the difference between David Beckham and a supermarket trolley?
A: A supermarket trolley has got a mind of its own.

*

POSH and Becks are sitting in front of the television watching the six o'clock news. The main story is a man threatening to jump off the Clifton Suspension Bridge onto the busy road below.

Posh turns to Becks and says: 'David, I bet you £5,000 that he jumps!' to which Beckham replies '£5,000? Done! I bet that he doesn't.' So they shake hands on the bet and continue watching.

Sure enough, the man jumps and hits the road below with a loud thud. Beckham takes £5,000 out of his back pocket and hands it to Posh. But she refuses.

> **SPORT**

'I can't take your money, David,' she says. 'The truth is, I was cheating. I saw the five o'clock news, so I knew he was going to jump.'

'No, babe,' says David. 'That money is yours fair and square. I was cheating just as you were. I saw the five o'clock news, too. I just didn't think he would do it again.'

——————————— Original Message ———————————

```
From: willis
To: webbo
Sent: Thursday, November 23, 2000 1:07 PM
Subject: FW: Golf love?
```

A man and a woman meet on holiday and quickly fall in love. At the end of the trip, they decide to open up to each other.
'It's only fair to warn you, Jill,' says Bob. 'I'm a golf nut. I live, eat, sleep and breathe golf.'
'Well, I'll be honest, too,' says Jill. 'I'm a hooker.'
The man looks crestfallen for a moment, then says, 'Are you keeping your wrists straight?'

THE WORLD'S GREATEST EMAIL JOKE BOOK

─────────── Original Message ───────────

```
From: webbo
To: willis
Sent: Monday, January 22, 2001 11:46 AM
Subject: FW: Sports quotes
```

'You don't like to see hookers going down on players like that.'

'He's looking for some meaningful penetration into the backline.'

'Spencer's running across field calling out, "Come inside me, come inside me."'

'I can tell you, it's a magnificent sensation when the gap opens up like that and you just burst right through.'

'I don't like this new law, because your first instinct when you see a man on the ground is to go down on him.'

'Darryl Gibson has been quite magnificent coming inside Andrew Mehrtens, and I'm looking forward to seeing more of the same today.'

'There's nothing that a tight forward likes more than a loosie right up his backside.'

SPORT

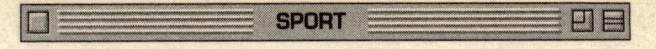

'Everybody knows that I have been pumping Martin Leslie for a couple of seasons now.'

──────────── Original Message ────────────

From: webbo
To: willis
Sent: Wednesday, April 24, 2002 5:13 PM
Subject: FW: Golfing tips

This sign was posted at a local golf club:

1. Back straight, knees bent, feet shoulder-width apart.
2. Form a loose grip.
3. Keep your head down.
4. Avoid a quick back swing.
5. Stay out of the water.
6. Try not to hit anyone.
7. If you are taking too long, please let others go ahead of you.
8. Don't stand directly in front of others.
9. Quiet please, while others are preparing to go.
10. Don't take extra strokes.

Well done. Now flush the urinal, go outside and tee off!

THE WORLD'S GREATEST EMAIL JOKE BOOK

———————— Original Message ————————

From: webbo
To: willis
Sent: Thursday, October 09, 2003 4:25 PM
Subject: FW: Come on you Spurs!

A seven-year-old boy was at the centre of a courtroom drama today when he challenged a court ruling over who should have custody of the boy.

The boy has a history of being beaten by his parents and the judge awarded custody to his aunt. The boy confirmed that his aunt beat him more than his parents did and refused to live there.

When the judge suggested that he live with his grandparents the boy cried out that they beat him more than anyone. The judge made the dramatic decision of allowing the boy to choose who should have custody of him.

Custody was yesterday granted to Tottenham Hotspur Football Club, as the boy firmly believes that they are not capable of beating anyone.

'Spurs are being predicted to stay in the Premiership for three more seasons: autumn, winter, spring...'

SPORT

'Glenn Hoddle went to the Spurs Christmas party last season dressed as a pumpkin. Come midnight, he still hadn't turned into a coach.

'Glenn Hoddle was wheeling his shopping trolley across the supermarket car park when he noticed an old lady struggling with her bags of shopping. He stopped and asked, 'Can you manage, dear?' To which the old lady replied, 'Sod off, mate. You got yourself into this mess. Don't ask me to sort it out!'

A Spurs fan walks into a pub with his dog just as the football scores appear on the TV screen. The announcer says that Spurs lost 3–0 and the dog immediately rolls over on to its back, sticks its paws in the air and plays dead.
'That's amazing,' says the barman. 'What does he do when they win?'
The Spurs fan scratches his head for a couple of minutes and finally replies, 'I dunno… I've only had the dog for eight months.'

Glenn Hoddle was caught speeding on his way to White Hart Lane at the weekend. 'I'll do anything for three points,' he said when questioned by police.

THE WORLD'S GREATEST EMAIL JOKE BOOK

The fire brigade phones Glenn Hoddle in the early hours of Sunday morning.
'Mr Hoddle, sir. White Hart Lane is on fire!'
'The cups, man! Save the cups!' cries Glenn.
'Uh, the fire hasn't spread to the canteen yet, sir...'

———————— Original Message ————————

From: webbo
To: willis
Sent: Sunday, June 27, 2004 11:05 AM
Subject: FW: Guess what's...

...just landed in my garden? Beckham's penalty!

	SPORT	

---— Original Message ———

From: willis
To: webbo
Sent: Monday, March 24, 2003 6:11 PM
Subject: FW: Beckham

David Beckham decides to go horse riding. Although he has had no previous experience, he skilfully mounts the horse and appears to be in complete command of the situation as the horse gallops along at a steady pace, while Victoria watches her husband admiringly.

After a short time David becomes a little casual and he begins to lose his grip in the saddle. He panics and grabs the horse around the neck shouting for it to stop. Victoria starts to scream and shout for someone to help her husband, as by this time David has slipped out of the saddle completely and is only saved from hitting the ground by the fact that he still has a grip on the horse's neck.

David decides that his best chance is to leap away from the horse, but his foot has become entangled in one of the stirrups. As the horse gallops along David's head is banging on the ground and he is slipping into unconsciousness. Victoria is now frantic and screams and screams for help! Hearing her screams, the Tesco security guard comes out of the store and unplugs the horse.

---------- Original Message ----------

From: webbo
To: willis
Sent: Friday, June 21, 2002 3:46 PM
Subject: FW: What could have happened...

If Beckham scores, we drink Becks.
If Scholes scores, we drink Skol.
If Mills scores, we drink Miller.
Thank f**k Seaman is in goal.

SPORT

———————— Original Message ————————

From: willis
To: webbo
Sent: Monday, February 12, 2001 11:13 AM
Subject: FW: Golfing accident

A couple of women were playing golf one sunny Saturday morning. The first of the twosome teed off and watched in horror as her ball headed directly towards a foursome of men playing the next hole. Indeed, the ball hit one of the men, and he immediately clasped his hands together at his crotch, fell to the ground and proceeded to roll around in evident agony. The woman rushed down to the man and immediately began to apologise. 'Please allow me to help,' she said. 'I'm a physical therapist and I know I could relieve your pain, if you'd allow.'

'Ummph, oooh, nnooo, I'll be all right… I'll be fine in a few minutes,' he replied breathlessly, as he remained in the foetal position still clasping his hands together at his crotch. But she persisted, and he finally allowed her to help him. She gently took his hands away and laid them to the side. She loosened his trousers, put her hands inside and began to massage him. 'How does that feel?' she asked. To which he replied, 'It feels great, but my hand still hurts like hell.'

THE WORLD'S GREATEST EMAIL JOKE BOOK

──────── Original Message ────────

From: webbo
To: willis
Sent: Wednesday, May 23, 2001 9:35 AM
Subject: FW: Liverpool v Man City

A primary teacher starts a new job at a school in Merseyside and, trying to make a good impression on her first day, explains to her class that she is a Liverpool fan. She asks her students to raise their hands if they, too, are Liverpool fans. Everyone in the class raises their hand except one little girl. The teacher looks at the girl with surprise and says, 'Mary, why didn't you raise your hand?'

'Because I'm not a Liverpool fan,' she replies.

The teacher, still shocked, asks, 'Well, if you're not a Liverpool fan, then who are you a fan of?'

'I'm a Manchester City fan, and proud of it,' says Mary.

The teacher can't believe her ears. 'Mary, why are you a City fan?'

'Because my mum and dad are from Manchester, and my mum is a City fan and my dad is a City fan, so I'm a City fan too!'

'Well,' says the teacher, obviously annoyed, 'that's no reason for you to be a City fan. You don't have to be just like your parents all of the time. What if your mum was a prostitute and your dad was a drug addict and car thief, what would you be then?'

'Then,' Mary smiled, 'I'd be a Liverpool fan.'

─────────────── Original Message ───────────────

```
From: willis
To: webbo
Sent: Friday, July 21, 2000 4:09 PM
Subject: FW: The van driver and the priest
```

A London van driver used to amuse himself by running over every Manchester United fan he would see strutting down the side of the road in their ubiquitous red colours. He would swerve to hit them, and there would be a loud THUMP, and then he would swerve back on the road.

One day, as the van driver was travelling along, he saw a priest hitchhiking. He thought he would do a good turn and pulled over. 'Where are you going, Father?' he asked.

'I'm going to say mass at St Joseph's church, about three kilometres down the road,' replied the priest.

'No problem, Father! I'll give you a lift. Climb in!'

The happy priest climbed into the passenger seat and the van continued down the road. Suddenly the driver saw a Manchester United fan walking along the pavement and instinctively swerved to hit him. But, just in time, he remembered the priest, so at the last minute he swerved back to the road, narrowly missing the man. However, even though he was certain he missed the glory-hunting idiot, he still heard a loud THUD. Not understanding where the noise came from, he glanced in his mirrors, and when he didn't see anything he turned to the priest and said, 'I'm sorry, Father, I almost hit the Manchester United fan.'

'That's OK,' replied the priest. 'I got the f**ker with the door!'

--- Original Message ---

From: webbo
To: willis
Sent: Thursday, June 10, 2004 2:02 PM
Subject: Euro 2004

David Beckham's voice is going to be used to make all stadium announcements at England's Euro 2004 matches. A spokesman said, 'We heard he comes over the PA really well.'

| | **SPORT** | |

---—— Original Message ——---

From: webbo
To: willis
Sent: Thursday, October 23, 2003 5:32 PM
Subject: FW: FW: If football teams were ladies...

Arsenal – Angelina Jolie. Looks good, a bit maverick at times, and you know they have the potential to really f**k you over.

Aston Villa – Dido. One big hit. Fairly inoffensive really.

Birmingham City – Mariah Carey. Occasionally interesting, frequently annoying. Supporters are thick.

Blackburn Rovers – Melanie Sykes. Common as muck, constantly worrying.

Bolton Wanderers – Natalie Imbruglia. Always looks like they might go down, but never do.

Charlton Athletic – Martine McCutcheon. Chirpy Cockney with the ability to spring a few surprises.

Chelsea – Maggie Thatcher. Hated by millions, supported by idiots.

Everton – Barbara Windsor. Been laughing at those tits so long, we forget that once upon a time they actually looked quite good!

Fulham – Andrea Corr. Not bad to look at, but not much of them. Seem a bit awestruck with fame.

Leicester City – Patsy Palmer. Generally a bit crap and second-rate, but some people like them.

Leeds United – Christina Aguilera. Dirrrty.

Liverpool – Sophie Ellis Bextor. Individually all the components look fantastic – just doesn't work when put together.

Manchester City – Madonna. Has been big at times; now an aging star that's lost the plot a bit. Nice new home, though.

Manchester United – Jordan. Dominated by tits. Quite repulsive, really.

Middlesbrough – Tara Palmer Tompkinson. Can look quite good at the back, but nothing at all up front to speak of.

SPORT

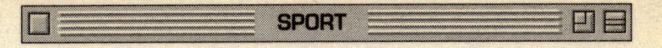

Newcastle United – Pamela Anderson. Can look good. Various unsavoury elements, though.

Portsmouth – Chrissie Hynde. On the face of it, a has-been, but you're quite interested in what they're going to do next.

Southampton – Kylie Minogue. Sometimes you feel sorry for them. They're not huge and you've got a bit of a soft spot.

Tottenham Hotspur – Kim Wilde. Glamorous in the '80s; not so nice to watch now.

Wolverhampton Wanderers – Lynda Lovelace. Big in the '70s; guaranteed to go down.

🢂 Travel

---——— Original Message ———---

From: willis
To: webbo
Sent: Tuesday, April 24, 2001 10:14 PM
Subject: FW: Airline humour

A plane was taking off from Kennedy Airport, New York City. After it reached a comfortable cruising altitude, the captain made an announcement over the intercom: 'Ladies and gentlemen, this is your captain speaking. Welcome to flight number 293, non-stop from New York to Los Angeles. The weather ahead is good and therefore we should have a smooth and uneventful flight. Now sit back and relax… OH, MY GOD!'

Silence followed and after a few minutes the captain came back on the intercom and said, 'Ladies and gentlemen, I am so sorry if I scared you earlier, but while

I was talking the flight attendant brought me a cup of coffee and spilled the hot coffee in my lap. You should see the front of my pants!'

A little old man at the back said, 'He should see the back of mine.'

TRAVEL

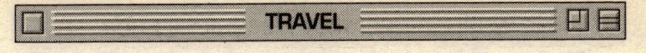

──────── Original Message ────────

From: webbo
To: willis
Sent: Friday, May 10, 2002 10:51 AM
Subject: FW: Toilet talk

Driving from Cambridge to London, I decided to make a stop at a motorway service station, where I went to the toilets. The first cubicle was taken so I went to the second one. I'd just sat down when I heard a voice from the next cubicle: 'Hi there, how's it going?' Now I'm not the type to strike up conversations with strangers in service station toilets. I didn't know what to say, but finally I said, 'Not bad…' Then the voice said, 'So, what are you doing?' I thought that was a little weird, but I said, 'Well, I'm just going to the toilet, then I'm heading down to London - '

'Look,' the voice interrupted, 'I'm gonna have to call you back. Every time I ask you a question, this idiot in the next cubicle keeps answering me!'

THE WORLD'S GREATEST EMAIL JOKE BOOK

──────────── Original Message ────────────

From: willis
To: webbo
Sent: Monday, June 10, 2002 4:17 PM
Subject: FW: Flight gaffes

All too rarely, airline attendants make an effort to make the in-flight 'safety lecture' and their other announcements a bit more entertaining. Here are some real examples that have been heard or reported:

On a flight with a very 'senior' flight-attendant crew, the pilot said, 'Ladies and gentlemen, we've reached cruising altitude and will be turning down the cabin lights. This is for your comfort and to enhance the appearance of your flight attendants.'

On landing, the stewardess said, 'Please be sure to take all your belongings. If you're going to leave anything, please make sure it's something we'd like to have.'

'There may be 50 ways to leave your lover, but there are only four ways to leave the aircraft.'

'Thank you for flying with us. We hope you enjoyed giving us the business as much as we enjoyed taking you for a ride.'

TRAVEL

As the plane landed and was coming to a stop at Washington National, a lone voice came over the loudspeaker: 'Whoa, big fella. WHOA!'

After a particularly rough landing during thunderstorms in Memphis, a flight attendant announced, 'Please take care when opening the overhead compartments because, after a landing like that, sure as hell everything has shifted.'

From another employee: 'Welcome aboard this flight XXX to YYY. To operate your seat belt, insert the metal tab into the buckle and pull tight. It works just like every other seat belt; and if you don't know how to operate one, you probably shouldn't be out in public unsupervised.'

'In the event of a sudden loss of cabin pressure, masks will descend from the ceiling. Stop screaming, grab the mask and pull it over your face. If you have a small child travelling with you, secure your mask before assisting them with theirs. If you are travelling with more than one small child, pick your favourite.'

'Your seat cushions can be used for flotation, and in the event of an emergency water landing, please paddle to shore and take them with our compliments.'

'Weather at our destination is 50 degrees with some broken clouds, but we'll try to have them fixed before we arrive. Thank you, and remember – nobody loves you, or your money, more than we do.'

A plane was making its descent into Amarillo, Texas, on a particularly windy and bumpy day. During the final approach, the captain really had to fight the turbulence. After an extremely hard landing, the flight attendant said, 'Ladies and gentlemen, welcome to Amarillo. Please remain in your seats with your seat belts fastened while the captain taxis what's left of our plane to the gate!'

'Should the cabin lose pressure, oxygen masks will drop from the overhead area. Please place the bag over your own mouth and nose before assisting children ... or other adults acting like children.'

And from the pilot during his welcome message: 'We are pleased to have some of the best flight attendants in the industry. Unfortunately, none of them are on this flight!'

Another flight attendant's comment on a less-than-perfect landing: 'We ask you to please remain seated as Captain Kangaroo bounces us to the terminal.'

An airline pilot wrote that, on this particular flight, he had

hammered his ship into the runway really hard. The airline had a policy that required the first officer to stand at the door while the passengers exited, smile and give them a 'Thanks for flying with XXX Airline.' He said that, in light of his bad landing, he had a hard time looking the passengers in the eye, thinking that someone would have a smart comment. Finally everyone had got off the plane except for a little old lady walking with a cane. She said, 'Sonny, mind if I ask you a question?'
'Why no, ma'am,' said the pilot. 'What is it?'
'Did we land or were we shot down?'

After a plane made a very hard landing in Salt Lake City, the flight attendant came on the intercom and said, 'That was quite a bump, and I know what y'all are thinking. I'm here to tell you it wasn't the airline's fault, it wasn't the pilot's fault, it wasn't the flight attendant's fault… It was the asphalt!'

'As you exit the plane, be sure to gather all of your belongings. Anything left behind will be distributed evenly among the flight attendants. Please do not leave children or spouses.'

After a real crusher of a landing in Phoenix, Arizona, the flight attendant announced, 'Ladies and gentlemen, please remain in your seats until Captain Crash and the crew have brought the aircraft to a screeching halt against the gate. And once the tyre smoke has cleared and the warning bells are silenced, we'll open the door and you can pick your way through the wreckage to the terminal.'

Part of a flight attendant's arrival announcement: 'We'd like to thank you folks for flying with us today. And the next time you get the insane urge to go blasting through the skies in a pressurised metal tube, we hope you'll think of us.'